THE WHEELS OF TIME II

The wheels keep turning.

Celebrating 250 Years

The Wheels of Time II by East Berlin Founder's Day Committee

ISBN 978-1-63452-297-7

Commemorating History
Est. May 8, 1764
CELEBRATE
250 YEARS
WITH US
East Berlin
Planning For The Future
BICENTENNIAL
1764
1964
EAST BERLIN, PA.

In the beginning God created the heaven and the earth. — Genesis 1:1.

And God said, Let the earth bring forth grass, the herb yielding seed, and the fruit tree yielding fruit after his kind . . . Genesis 1:11

And God created . . . every living creature that moveth . . . Genesis 1:21

And God blessed them, saying, Be fruitful, and multiply . . . Genesis 1:22

. . . God created man in his own image . . . Genesis 1:27

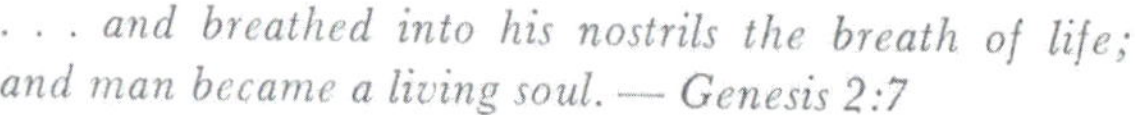

. . . and breathed into his nostrils the breath of life; and man became a living soul. — Genesis 2:7

. . . and God said unto them, Be fruitful and multiply, and replenish the earth . . . Genesis 1:28

Thus the heavens and the earth were finished, and all the host of them.

And on the seventh day God ended his work which he had made; and he rested on the seventh day from all his work which he had made.

And God blessed the seventh day and sanctified it: because that in it he had rested from all his work which God created and made. — Genesis 2:1-3

Wheels of time . . .

As the earth was formed and turned on its axis, we had the beginning of time. Let no man misconstrue his destiny in time.

We are born, and we pass on. The existence of a man is told in what he is. As history passes us, we look toward the future; eventually, *that* becomes our past. So it has been with man on earth, in our nation, and in our own community.

As the wheels of time turn and leave their tracks on the earth, so man leaves his mark on the lives of those around him. Time itself erases many tracks, but those of significance and beauty remain to be appreciated. Even the tracks of sorrow linger to be felt by man of today and tomorrow. Life does not exist for pleasure alone; but to know pleasure, we must know life. Time alone is man's own teacher.

With the wheels of time carrying us through this book, we may receive a better understanding of what time has taught us and what man of today can do to create tracks which will be of memorable significance to our community, as the wheels move on to their final destiny.

TABLE OF CONTENTS

In the grand scheme of life, 50 years isn't all that long, only a couple of generations in one family at the most. In the life of the Borough of East Berlin and its surrounding communities, 50 years is an eternity in terms of how the community has grown, evolved, and changed.

In 1964, a committee of dedicated individuals published a book The Wheels of Time to commemorate and celebrate the first 200 years of East Berlin. The current Founder's Day Committee was established in 2013 with the goal of planning and holding events to celebrate the 250th Anniversary of East Berlin's Founding. On May 1-11, 2014, the Founder's Day Committee of the East Berlin Borough held events to celebrate the 250th Anniversary of East Berlin's founding on May 8, 1764.

In addition to those events, the second goal of the Founder's Day Committee was to produce a new book to commemorate the 50 years since the original book. This book, *The Wheels of Time II: The Wheels Keep Turning* incorporates sections of the original 1964 Wheels of Time book that are still pertinent to our history today. These original pages have been professionally scanned from the original book and are designated with a border in this book with a special logo. Each section in *Wheels of Time II* will also be updated with information on the happenings in town of the last 50 years. These pages are in full color and are after the 1964 pages in each section.

BICENTENNIAL EAST BERLIN, PA QUILT

Jeannie Gross, Grace Cook, Mary Crone, Fern King, (Sarah Hothan lives in Nebraska and is not in the picture)

The Quilt was made for the June 1964 Bicentennial and was designed by Irwin Gross (Jeannie's father) and was sewn by Irwin's sister Florence A. Hull. Grace, Mary, Fern and Sarah are Florence's daughters. The quilt is lovingly kept by Jeannie Gross in pristine condition.

The symbols in the quilt represent the following:

Cross *- the local churches*

Wheels *- the Wheels of Time*

Flag *- Country*

Keystone and Flower *- State and State Flower*

Plow*- Swords into Plow Shares (the pageant that was performed in 1964)*

Torch *- For the Olympics that was held in 1964*

Rifle, fishing rod and baseball *- the recreational activities that are held in the area.*

You may be asking what has changed to prompt another book. Well, the short answer is that the Borough of East Berlin and its surrounding communities has changed. We now have a public library that will soon be expanding to provide even better services to the community. We have a Community Center that supports the recreational and community outreach needs. We have a Lions Club and VFW who do important work in service of our town. The library and community center didn't exist during the 200th celebration so we are really excited to document their histories now. The VFW and Lions Club have grown so much since the 1964 book so their new deeds will also be documented.

The other obvious way our lives have changed in the last fifty years is the way we use technology in every part of our daily lives. Take the Wheels of Time book for example. Each page of that book was painstakingly laid out piece by piece so it could be sent off to the printing company who then compiled it in a book. Today the process is much the same, but totally different in certain ways. For *Wheels of Time II*, Andi Simpson, our graphic design expert laid out all of the pages, text, and photos digitally and we will email the final draft off to the publishers to be produced. In addition to Andi Simpson, we would also like to thank two individuals who were instrumental in taking digital photographs for the new book. Loy Elliott and Donald Dixon volunteered their efforts to take pictures of every event the Founder's Day Committee held this year. Without their help, Wheels of Time II would not have been produced. Sadly, we aren't quite sure which process took longer, but we are hoping it was the 1964 edition of the book.

To finish, we present the original words of The Wheels of Time, slightly updated for the new book: "To the community we present ***The Wheels of Time II***: *The Wheels Keep Turning* on the occasion of our Sestercentennial anniversary, 2014."

Roberta Teal,
Committee President

Brandt A. Ensor

Charles Bechtel

Mary Beth LeVan

Wayne Lau

Hannelore Furst

William Mayer

Annie Deardorff,
(Also Known as Leslie Deardorff's Daughter)

Sue Hilbert

Robin Heyser

Karen Wire

In creating this book, the Founder's Day Committee canvassed the community's organizations and businesses asking for their histories, specifically since 1964. Their responses largely make up the business and service sections of this book.

BEFORE OUR TIME

Today near our springs and streams one can find evidences of crude stone tools. Arrow heads, spears, knives, tomahawks, celts, axes, skinners, mortars and pestles are artifacts that may be the remains of night-camp sites used by the Indians when they traveled to and from war; many of them are remains from hunting parties and the small settled camps.

The names that are familiar to us when we refer to some of our streams are derivations of the Iroquois Confederation and Iroquoian language. Our own *Conewago* and *Bermudian* Creeks bear these Indian connotations. As we look at a map and find other names such as *Conowingo*, *Codorus*, and even the word *Conestoga* — which was the name taken by the last remnants of the Susquehannock tribe in Lancaster — indicate the lasting influence of the Indian in this area.

1964 Original Pages

The first settlers that found their way into Adams County discovered this to be an ideal area for the wildlife native to Pennsylvania. The Indian, too, found these lands ideal for hunting, because of the abundance of wildlife.

In this era, the Indians' nature was similar to that of the wildlife; they were nomadic by nature and found little use or value in settling in one area. This area being one of their better hunting grounds, it was used almost exclusively for that purpose. Their primary value of glory was acquired through war. War among different tribes and nations was quite common. If we had a way of learning all of the historical data about the Indians, we might be amazed to find that this area had been a great Indian battlefield. The abundance of Indian relics found in nearby areas supports our belief that many lived and fought here.

The total Indian population in Pennsylvania has been estimated to have been approximately fifteen to twenty thousand in the seventeenth century. The population increased as the tribes such as the Shawnee and Tuscarora moved in from the south, after being driven out by white settlers and Indian wars.

The Susquehannock Indian Nation was the most prominent of the Indian tribes in this area. They were a detached band of Iroquois Indians that became independent of the Iroquois Confederation and became hated enemies of their former tribesmen. The Susquehannock lived along the Susquehanna River and its tributaries; they lived in small groups of fifty to one hundred for about twenty years. After their land became unproductive and the game grew scarce, they moved to another area. Since the early Indians did not have a beast of burden, they depended upon their ability to transport their few possessions by waterway. Therefore, only occasionally a group would come as far west of the Susquehanna as the East Berlin community. Most of those that came to this area were outcasts from a tribe; they moved in an effort to find a remote area where they could live in peace.

In 1663, only one hundred years before the founding of Berlin, the Susquehannock defeated and repulsed an attack on their territory by the Seneca and Cayuga tribes. However, four years later the Susquehannock Nation felt the effects of continuous war and sickness; emissaries were sent to the Five Nations of the Iroquois Confederation in an attempt to make peace. The enraged Iroquois refused to "smoke the pipe of peace," and hostilities continued until most of the Susquehannock were either captured or slain. The remnants of this tribe and those of the Delaware tribe of the eastern part of Pennsylvania were the Indians that settled in this area, the cause of most of the early settlers' difficulties.

In 1682, William Penn organized the three original Counties of Pennsylvania — Philadelphia, Bucks and Chester. Quickly, the area of settlement expanded; and on May 19, 1729, it was considered necessary to establish a county government for the area settled in the westerly part of Chester County. This was named Lancaster County. As the settlements moved still westward, the jurisdiction of this fourth County was extended to include the area of present-day Adams County.

The opening of this area was finally made safe by the purchase of a large area west of the Susquehanna River from the Indians in 1736. But even before the purchase, settlers had come over the River to give some semblance of claim to the lands settled; and through the Pennsylvania authorities, authorized Samuel Blunston to issue warrants after 1729.

As the area settled included present-day Adams County, some of the earliest land holdings were Blunston licenses. The earliest records found to indicate the first settlement in present-day Adams County were those of 1734. The Irish, the Dutch, the Germans and the English (Quakers) mark the separate nationalities that sent immigrants into the community. Industry and religion were the "strong marks" of all the early settlers. The descendants of these brave old pioneers who are so fortunate as to possess, to this day, one of the spots where the smoke of the first cabin of their ancestors rose upon "the unvexed air," may well regard it as hallowed ground.

In 1749, the settlements west of the Susquehanna River having multiplied, and the population of those parts having increased considerably, another county government was considered necessary; York County was organized on August 19, 1749. This also included the area now known as Adams County. This was the fifth County of Pennsylvania and the first located west of the Susquehanna River. Each resident contributed to the best of his ability, the men felled the trees, the women and children gathered and burned the brush. Their food was simple, but they attacked it with enormous appetites. Even with a full day's work, there was no time when their family worship was neglected. Their Bible and Prayer Books were all the books they had to read. As soon as there were five or six families that could call each other neighbors, they commenced the effort of a church and schoolhouse; one building served both purposes.

The parental authority was unbending, and when they read in their Bibles, *children be obedient to your parents,* this became a stern religious obligation. Their lives were too earnest to be frivolous. They prayed more than they laughed. Their thoughts and conversation were divided between bread in this world and heaven in the next. They lived next to the earth in most respects, and they knew the true meaning of the phrase, *The Good Earth.*

But soon came children, weddings, more homes, pack peddlars with wares to sell and news to relate from the outside world. And then came the town at the crossroads with its store, blacksmith shop, wagon maker's shop, and grist mill if water was near; and with this came John Frankenburger, of German ancestry, and the town of *Berlin.*

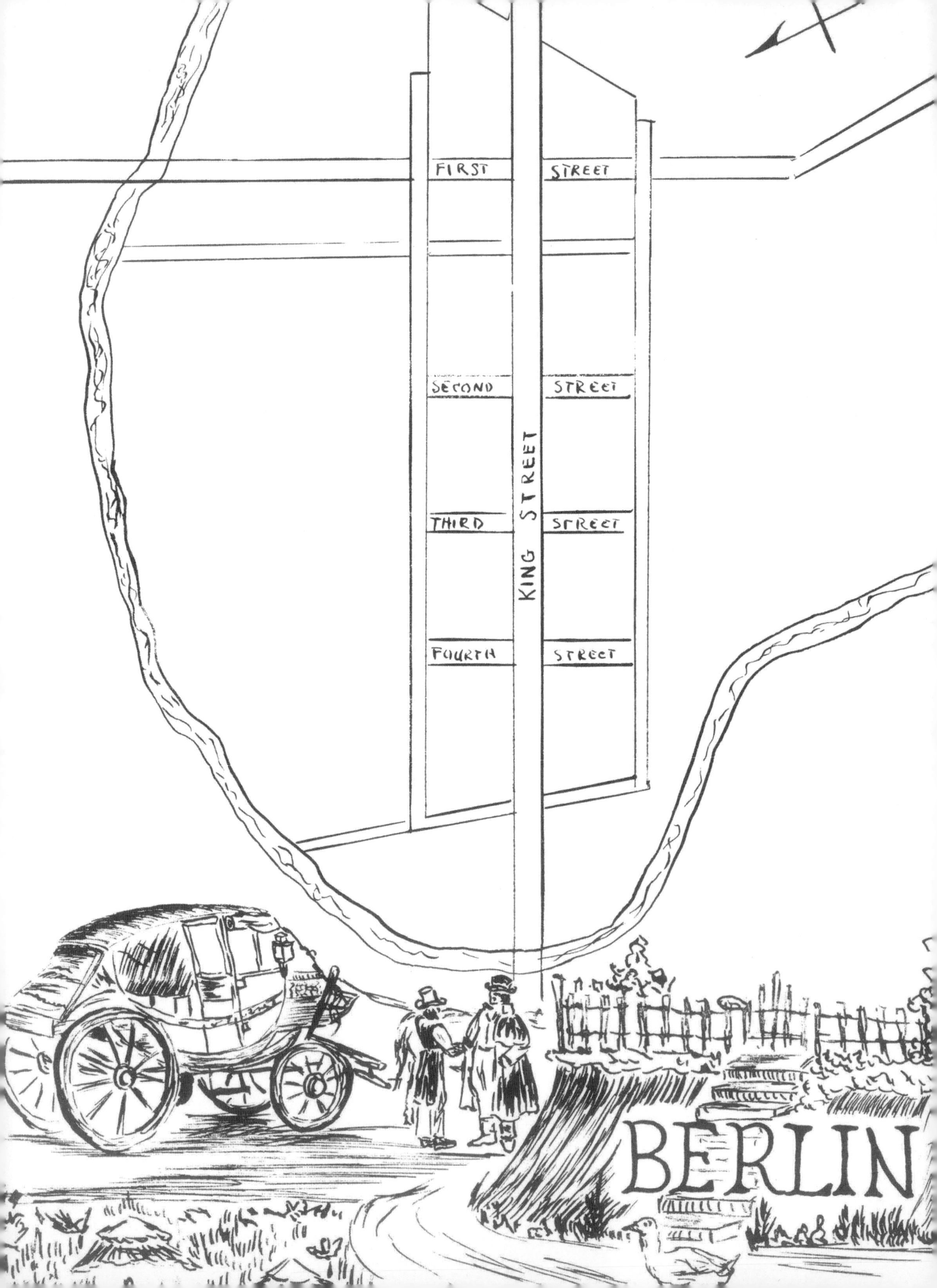
FIRST STREET
SECOND STREET
THIRD STREET
FOURTH STREET
KING STREET
BERLIN

BERLIN

Map of 1770

East Berlin, *a Borough having a population of 1033* according to the 1960 census, is situated in the southeastern part of Adams County. At one time, the Borough was a part of Hamilton Township — formerly Berwick Township — York County, and is situated at the junction of the Conewago and Beaver Creeks. East Berlin is located four miles from Abbotstown, ten from Hanover, six from New Oxford, thirteen from York, eighteen from Gettysburg, fourteen from Dillsburg and fifty-two from Baltimore.

The American Gazetteer of 1797 refers to Berlin as follows: *Berlin is a near and flourishing town of York County, Pennsylvania, containing about 100 houses. It is regularly laid out on the southwestern side of the Conewago Creek, thirteen miles westerly of Yorktown and one hundred one west of Philadelphia in north latitude 39 degrees 56 minutes.*

While there are several pretentious hills in the vicinity of East Berlin, there are no mountainous tracts. The soil is red gravel, flinty and very productive. The surface rolls heavily in parts, but large tracts of comparatively level land exist. The elevation of East Berlin above the Atlantic level is 550 feet. Pine Hill, near East Berlin, just north of the "Conowago" Creek, which borders the entire north and western part of the town, contains a mineral resembling umber.

John Frankenberger, a Prussian, purchased two hundred acres of land, from Thomas and Richard Penn, for which he paid 28 pounds, 16 shillings and 7 pence, amounting to approximately $80.71 today; and on the eighth day of May, 1764 laid out the town into 85 lots, with one main street, four cross streets and five alleys. He called the new town *Berlin,* after his native place in the Fatherland. *East* was added when the post office was established, to distinguish it from another *Berlin* in the State of Pennsylvania.

The cost of lots was two pounds fifteen shillings each, amounting to approximately $7.70 today. Every purchaser was required to erect a dwelling house on each lot within two years and six months — the house to be at least twenty feet in length and sixteen in breadth, with either a stone or brick chimney attached. If the houses were not built in said time, the lot or lots were forfeited to the original owner. Purchasers were required to pay on each lot a yearly rent of one Spanish dollar, or the value thereof in Pennsylvania currency, to the said Frankenberger or his heirs. On May 16, 1774 Mr. Frankenberger disposed of his interest to Peter Househill for the sum of 550 pounds, who reserved lots #64 and #65 for himself. Mr. Househill sold his interest to Andrew Comfort on March 18, 1782.

At Mr. Comfort's death, his last will and testament ordered and directed, *that his wife, the said Mary Elizabeth Comfort should have the one third of his personal estate, and privilege to live in one of the Store Rooms and privilege to Kook in the Kitching, and to put her nefsesaryes in the Sellar, and to have the new Gardin and a piece of Ground for Potatoes during her life, and son Andrew to have the land if he pays 1300 lb.* The will was dated November 19, 1789. Andrew accepted and sold the property to John Hildebrand, Sr. on January 21, 1794.

Mr. Hildebrand laid out 100 more lots on the north side of town, known as *Hildebrand's Addition* to the original town of *Berlin*.

EARLY HOMES OF BERLIN

These are some of the homes built before 1800. The present property owners have made attempts to search early records relative to past owners, construction date and historical data; but the records gave only vague impressions of some homes while interesting history was found regarding some of the other homes.

Robert B. Jacobs: Approximately 200 years old

Oscar and Sarah E. Reynolds: Lot #83. Reserved by Frankenberger for his use.

Lewis D. Spangler: Built May 1, 1789, Lots 80-81-82, owner has all original deeds, and all of the original building is still in use.

Mrs. Thomas Straley: Believed to be the first home built in Berlin.

Glenn Weaver: Built before 1790; all of the original building remains; used as a tannery between 1790-1800.

Roy Weigard: Built in 1790, all of the original structure remains except the porches.

In 1800, the increase in population of York County made it necessary to sub-divide the county. Adams County was then organized January 22, 1800 and became the twenty-sixth county organized in Pennsylvania. The new County contained 526 square miles or 336,640 acres with a population of 13,172.

Adams County was named for John Adams, the second President of the United States — 1797-1801, who was greatly admired by the residents of the County.

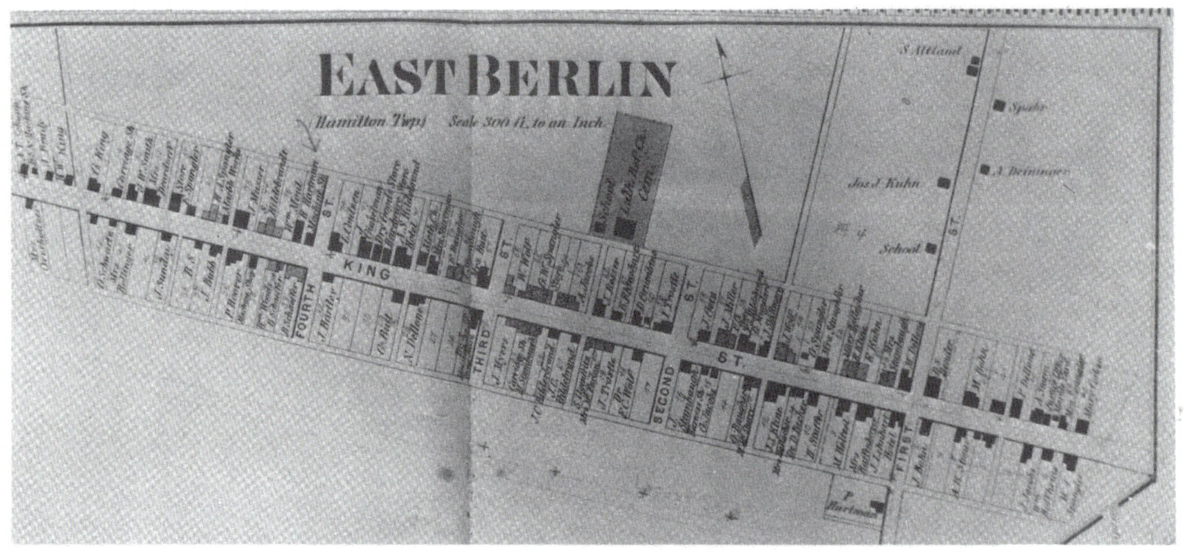

East Berlin, Adams County, 1872

During the year 1879, the people of Hamilton Township, of which East Berlin formed a part, became dissatisfied with having the election poll in East Berlin and petitioned the court to have it moved to Pine Run Schoolhouse, about three miles from town. An election was held accordingly, at which time it was decided to move the poll to Pine run. When the fall election occurred, the citizens of East Berlin turned out "en masse;" and headed by the Berlin Band, proceeded to the new election poll to deposit their ballots. As a consequence, the people of East Berlin petitioned the Court of Adams County to incorporate their town into a borough. The petition was approved, and East Berlin became an incorporated Borough on November 10, 1879. After approval of the petition by the court, the land was surveyed and was found to contain *Four Hundred and Seven (407) Acres neat measure.*

By order of the Court of Adams County, the Annual Borough Election shall be held at the 'Old School House,' known as 'the Church School House,' on the Third Tuesday of February.

and believe that it is expedient to grant the prayer of the petitioners

A. P. Starr
Foreman

In the matter of the Incorporation of the Town of East Berlin

Decree of Court

And now to wit: November 10, A. D. 1879 The Court Confirm the judgment of the Grand Jury and Decree that the said town of East Berlin be incorporated into a Borough in conformity with the prayer of the petitioners, that the Corporate style and title thereof shall be the "Borough of East Berlin," that the boundaries thereof shall be as follows to wit: Beginning at a point (Stones), on the banks of Conewago Creek on lands of Widow Hollinger, thence by lands of same and heirs of B. Hil-

The first election was held accordingly on February 17, 1880, with the following persons duly elected to the several offices of said Borough: *Burgess,* George King; *Town Council,* John Hartley, Jacob Resser, Michael Rebert, George W. Baugher, Henry Shafer and John Weist; *School Directors,* William S. Hildebrand, Edward Shaffer, Robert N. Meisenhelder, J. Harry Bohn, William B. Moul, Simon Altland; *Assessor,* John Getz; *Judge,* Henry L. Miller; *Inspectors,* Michael Helsel, F. S. Hildebrand; *Justice of the Peace,* Albert W. Storm, Luther Y. Diller; *Auditor,* C. W. Stoner; *Constable,* Emanual Rhinehart.

On February 23, 1880 members of Town Council — elect met at the office of A. W. Storm, Esquire; and after duly sworn according to law, organized by calling the Burgess to the chair. After appointing John Picking as secretary, they adjourned to meet at the *Church School House* on Saturday the thirteenth day of March, A. D. 1880 at 1:00 p.m. At this meeting, a committee was appointed to confer with the Board of Trustees of the *Church School House* in regard to renting it for the term of one year *for meetings of Town Council* and to agree on the amount of rent for same. It was noted that at one place under "payment of bills," there was an item of $7 to the Board of Trustees of *Church School House* for rent for one year. Council met on the second Friday of each month at 1:00 p.m.

The most-pressing problems were cared for first; and, without a doubt, stones, curbs, crosswalks, gutters, sidewalks, provision and care of street lamps and the ever-unpopular ordinances for safety and protection of the citizens were at the top of the list.

. . . that no owner of any horses, mares, geldings, mules, swine, goats, cows, bulls, sheep, shall allow the same to run at large or be herded upon the public streets, alleys or public places of this Borough. (April 9, 1880)

. . . that if any person shall 'suffer' his or her cellar door or doors to remain open after dark on the public street, such person or persons shall, on conviction thereof before the Burgess for such 'offence,' be fined the sum of Fifty cents. (April 9, 1880)

. . . that it shall not be lawful for any person or persons to cut or dig sod on the Street or alley of the Borough. (April 9, 1880)

Burgess and Councilmen Jacob Resser and John Weist met. There being no quorum present, the Burgess ordered a special meeting for next Monday evening, May 16 — at 7½ o'clock. (May 13, 1881)

. . . On motion of J. R. Darone, Council agreed to purchase one dozen Street Lamps for this Borough. H. B. Jacobs then moved that the secretary be instructed to order one dozen Square Tubular Street Lamps with Extension Burners from Messers Cavitt & Pollock, Pittsburg. (September 15, 1883)

. . . An order (payment) was granted to H. G. Berkheimer for lighting lamps — 54 nights $8.10 and Mr. Berkheimer asked his salary to be increased. (November 6, 1884) The salary was raised to 20 cents per night provided the lamps were lit and kept in good care.

The number of taxpayers in the Borough of East Berlin (1886) as 243; value of real estate, $186,069; number of horses, etc., 72; of cows, etc., 33; value of money on interest, $94,631; value of trades and professions, $10,160; number of pleasure carriages, 63; of gold watches, 9; acres of timberland, 14.

. . . The clerk for the Boro Council stated he had called on C. K. Seifert for rent to have his 'car' on a street, and that Mr. Seifert said he was poor and unable to pay 25 cents per week. Council disposed of this matter by asking Mr. Seifert to pay $2.00 for rent to date and 'hereafter' to pay the sum of 12½ per week, and to move his 'car' as soon as he can. (January 20, 1887)

. . . the clerk stated that he received $1.00 for a permit from the Building Committee of the Lutheran Church to erect a church on Main Street. (November 11, 1887)

. . . A letter from Dr. John Weist was read, and, on motion of Mr. Tschop, was received and ordered to place it on file. Mr. Tschop made a motion that the council accept Dr. Weist's proposition and have the line put up at once, and if lights are as represented, to accept and pay the same, should the lights not be satisfactory, there should be no expense to the Borough for putting up said line, also that the clerk be ordered to write Dr. Wiest to that effect. (January 3, 1888)

The street committee selected positions for the light poles, and the poles were installed promptly.

. . . the lamps at the west end of town, as far down as Meisenhelder's Drug Store (later Noah Sprenkle's Hardware Store) *prove satisfactory but from there down to the east end they do not come up to standard. (January 3, 1888)*

A committee of two was appointed by Council to go back to York and *to see Dr. Wiest with regards to the lights and explain the dissatisfaction existing among the citizens.* Dr. Wiest promised immediately *to put them in good shape.* At the same meeting, a request was granted to place a light at Wehler's Blacksmith Shop and at Henry Shaffer's barn. Motions were made to pay Dr. Wiest for *electric lighting* for July and August — $20, and to pay William Blinsinger for burying beef head — 50 cents. (January 3, 1888)

Another notice appeared in the Council's records on December 26, 1888 concerning the lighting problem; this read: *repair the line within 10 days or return the Fifty Dollars as per agreement.* The record also indicated at this time that the Council would not buy the line as per Dr. Wiest's agreement.

According to the Council minutes of August 30, 1888, Dr. John Wiest was paid $20 for *electric lighting* for the months of September and October and that the secretary was to inform Dr. Wiest that he would receive no further pay for the *electric lights* unless they were put in good order.

. . . On motion by Mr. Butt the following orders were granted: (October 30, 1888)

Jacob Gulden — Labor on road	$ .50
H.B. Jacobs — Labor on road and team	12.50
Frank Kuhn — Labor on road	1.00
Henry Shaffer — Team Hire	.56
John Wehler — Sharpening tools	1.70

. . . Exhonorations granted (March 13, 1889)

George Baker	$ .15
William Blinsinger	.03
Charles Grove	.23
H. L. Miller	.13
Daniel Sell	.11

On May 1, 1889 a motion was made by Council that an Ordinance be passed to have boardwalks put down in front of all unimproved lots fronting streets to be replaced with brick or stone when improved.

S. Morgan Smith reported to the Burgess on August 6, 1889 *that as soon as he finds out the amount of power required to run his mill* (now the East Berlin Mill) *he would be ready to put in a bid to light the Borough.* A committee from the Town Council was appointed to *wait on* S. Morgan Smith.

On November 4, 1889 the committee reported that S. Morgan Smith declined to furnish power to run the *electric lights.*

. . . that we purchase thirty-one lights and ½ dozen extra globes. (December 2, 1889)

. . . special meeting to open proposals for lighting street lights.

John Stewart	50 cents per night for 30 lights; 25 cents for 15
J. R. Thoman	38 cents for 30 lights; 20 cents for 15
Israel Hartman	50 cents for 30 lights; 25 cents for 15
H. L. Miller	45 cents or $100 per year
W. F. Kuhn	35 cents
John Burgard	75 cents
Aamos Rhinehart	44 cents
Geo Emig	75 cents

W.F. Kuhn receiving the majority of votes was declared elected. (December 8, 1889)

. . . Agreed to sell the old street lights at 50¢ each. (January 6, 1891)

On April 7, 1891 the Burgess was ordered to sell the street-light poles at 30 cents each.

. . . On motion of Mr. Spangler, Council agreed to offer a reward of $100 for the arrest and conviction of the party or parties that fired the stable of Mrs. Moul or for any other fires that might occur in the future of (incendiary) origin, and that the secretary have 25 bills printed and posted up through town. (May 5, 1891)

. . . the time for lighting the lamps was fixed from 1st of May to September at 8 o'clock and extinguishing at 11 o'clock. (April 7, 1889)

. . . Council granted Mr. Howe permission to explain the workings of his combined Water and Chemical Fire Engine, after Mr. Butt made a motion, seconded by Mr. Nickey that Council purchase an Engine from Mr. Howe. Motion carried. A committee was appointed to make the purchase of an engine from Mr. Howe as cheap as possible. *(April 3, 1892)*

. . . A. B. Trimmer's bid of $1079.50 was accepted to build the engine house. (June 1, 1892) . . . (Dedicated engine house on October 22, 1892)

. . . Messers Spangler and Leas, Committee on Engine, reported that they waited on Mr. Howe and contracted with him for one of "their" Combined Engines with 25 feet Extra Suction Hose and 200 feet Extra Discharge Hose for $675, cash, delivered in East Berlin. (May 7, 1892)

. . . On motion of Mr. Baker, the secretary was ordered to notify J. Reigle to keep his cows off the main street to pasture but he may leav *them in the alleys if herded. (June 2, 1891)*

The reservoir was built in 1897; the engineer was Mr. Mengeringhausen. The water plant contract was awarded to Bolton G. Coon (Kingston, Pennsylvania) for a total of $8,792.55. This was financed by coupon bonds of the Borough of East Berlin in the amount of $9,700.

Land for the pump hose was purchased from Mr. Baugher for $250 per acre; one acre was purchased.

Digging the reservoir, 1897.

Land for the reservoir was purchased from Mrs. Geiselman for $100 per acre; one acre was purchased.

The reservoir is clay-tempered with the capacity of 500,000 gallons.

. . . Finance Committee reported that it sold the Band Wagon and the chemical apparatus for $18.55. Expense of sale was 45¢ letting a balance of $18.10. (December 1, 1901)

. . . Action on a request of C. G. Chronister to light the town with acetylene lights was deferred. (April 4, 1911)

. . . Mr. Kurzeweil of Electric Mfg. Co. of York was present and stated to Council that he would install an Electric Light Plant for the Borough, furnishing steam engine dynamo and machinery for the sum of $1790.00 or Gasoline Engine for $1650.00. (July 3, 1911)

. . . Motion to proceed with the Electric Light Plant for the Borough lost by 4 'yes' and 3 'no' but

Constructing the reservoir.

required 5 votes since it was a motion over the veto of the Burgess.

. . . Motion to grant Trolley Co. from York the privilege to come to East Berlin. The Franchise to be void if no work is done within six months. (March 21, 1912) The work was never started.

. . The York Telephone and Telegraph constructed lines and an exchange in 1912.

1964 Original Pages

. . . J. R. Thoman elected lamp lighter at 55¢ per night with instructions to fill the lamps in daytime and to have lamps lighted whenever it is necessary that is, if it is moonlight time but cloudy. (December 21, 1914)

. . . J. R. Thoman was appointed lamp lighter and water pumper at 55¢ per night for lamp lighting and $12.50 per month for water pumping. (January 21, 1914)

. . . Motion made to increase the pay of the lamp lighter to 70¢ per night. (June 4, 1917)

On January 3, 1921 J. R. Thoman was appointed commissioner, lamp lighter, and water pumper for $55 per month.

The East Berlin and Abbottstown Electric Light Company asked for a franchise to erect light poles and to sell stocks to construct lines in the Borough for furnishing current for street lighting and general use. This was granted; and by the end of the year of 1921, the town was using the convenience. (Today, the Metropolitan Edison Company furnishes the power.)

In 1933, natural gas was piped into East Berlin by the Gettysburg Gas Company. (Today, this service is provided by the Columbia Gas Company of Pennsylvania.)

Municipal Authority

The East Berlin Municipal Authority is body corporate, organized under the Municipal Authorities Act of 1945, P. L. 382, as amended, in accordance with the terms of an Ordinance of the East Berlin Borough Council. Its Certificate of Incorporation was issued by the Secretary of the Commonwealth of Pennsylvania on June 14, 1955. The governing body of the Authority consists of five members appointed by the Council of East Berlin Borough. The terms of the Board members are staggered so that the term of one member expires each year. Members may be reappointed. None of the members is a member of the Borough Council.

The first Board consisted of the following: C. D. Krout, Chairman; Raymond H. Fissel, Vice Chairman; John R. Wisler, Secretary; John S. Lehr, Treasurer; Harry B. Nell, Assistant Secretary-Treasurer.

The Authority undertook as its first project the construction of a sewage collection system, sewage treatment plant, pump station, force main and interceptor and outfall sewers to be leased to and operated by the Borough of East Berlin. Charles W. Wolf, Esquire, was named Solicitor, and William E. Sees, Jr., Harrisburg, Pennsylvania, was chosen as Consulting Engineer.

Plans and specifications for the project were prepared by Engineer Sees and subsequently approved by the Borough Council. The Authority then determined to finance the project by issuing $270,000 principal amount of Sewer Revenue Bonds and retained the firm of Saul, Ewing, Remick & Saul, Philadelphia, Pennsylvania, as Underwriter for the bonds. The Gettysburg National Bank, Gettysburg, Pennsylvania, was named as Trustee.

Bids for the Project were opened on December 20, 1955; and the low bidders for each of the three contracts were recorded as follows: Contract #1 — Construction of the sewage collection system — Maitland Brothers, Littlestown, Pennsylvania, the bid being $104,761. Contract #2 — Construction of the sewage treatment plan — Johnston Brothers, Shippensburg, Pennsylvania, the bid being $87,063.36. Contract #3 — Electrical Work for the sewage treatment plant — I. B. Abel-Son, York, Pennsylvania, at its bid of $5525.

On February 7, 1956 contracts were awarded to the aforementioned low bidders; and work on the different contracts began shortly thereafter.

As construction of the main lines through the Borough progressed, many difficulties were encountered. Much blasting was required in the rocky sections of the Borough. Several cave-ins occurred resulting in minor injuries to some workmen, but there were no major incidents. The entire project was finished in time to have the system in full operation by the early part of February, 1957. The system has been in successful operation since then and is a real asset to the Borough of East Berlin.

THE INCONVENIENCE OF PROGRESS

1964 Original Pages

Of the original Bond issue of $270,000, only $232, 000 are presently outstanding; $38,000 of the bonds having been paid (and cancelled) out of the Sewer rents collected since operations began.

Present members of the Authority Board are: C. D. Krout, Raymond H. Fissel, John R. Wisler, John S. Lehr, and Sherman B. Krall. Mr. Krall replaced Harry B. Nell who now resides in Reading Township. The financing of future Borough projects may be handled by the Authority when called upon to do so by the Borough Council.

East Berlin Borough, through its own municipally owned water works, serves the community residents with a public-water supply. The facility consists of: two drilled wells, a centrifugal-booster pump, a reservoir, elevated tank, chlorination and metering facilities, and a distribution system.

Drilled Well No. 1, located northwest of the corporate limits of the borough and adjacent to the reservoir, is 250 feet deep. The well is equipped with a 50 g.p.m. pump which discharges directly into the reservoir and is housed in a single story brick pump house.

Drilled Well No. 2, located in a brick structure just beyond the northwest Borough boundary line near the Conewago Creek, is 300 feet deep. This well is equipped with a 120 g.p.m. pump which can discharge into the reservoir or feed directly into the distribution system.

The storage reservoir, 20 to 30 feet east of Well Pump House No. 1, is a rectangular brick structure having a water depth of 12 feet and capacity of 500, 000 gallons.

In April, 1962 the Borough completed a $115,000 general-improvements program, which added a 150, 000 gallon steel elevated tank to the distribution system.

Under this program, a centrifugal-booster pump of 100 g.p.m. capacity was installed in Pump House No. 2. This pump feeds the distribution system and elevated storage tank.

Along with th elevated tank and booster pump, a new 10-inch cast iron feeder main was installed as an improvement to the distribution system. The 3½ miles of sub-main consists of 6" and 8" diameter pipe with a small percentage of 4" diameter pipe still in service.

The facilities maintain a fire flow through the industrial and commercial sections of the community at 1000 g.p.m. and provide a minimum service requirement of 500 g.p.m. to all residential sections.

The average daily water consumption through the 350 connections to the system amounts to approximately 50,000 gallons per day or 48 gallons per day per person.

The continued development and improvement of the community-owned public works facilities contributes largely to the growth and prosperity of the Borough of East Berlin.

A major secondary highway intersects at East Berlin. This is Pennsylvania State Highway Route No. 194 running north and south, and intersecting Route No. 234, running east and west.

adequate surface run-off during rains of maximum intensity.

As the Borough's participation in this Highway Construction Program, it was ordained that the new

The Borough portion of these highways, running north, south, east, and west, are being rebuilt curb to curb with a matching State and Federal Grant of $375,000. Work began on March 25, 1963.

Under this program, a new storm water drainage system was installed to provide the community with

highways be lined with concrete curbing from borough to borough line. This undertaking began in 1958, east and west, by individual property owners — north and south being completed as part of the Highway Construction Program, with costs being administered by the Borough under an assessment program.

POPULATION STATISTICS FOR EAST BERLIN

The population growth of East Berlin has been slow but steady through the years. The following population statistics show that the greatest increase has occurred during the last two decades:

1820 — 418
1880 — 510
1900 — 668
1920 — 610
1940 — 792
1960 — 1033

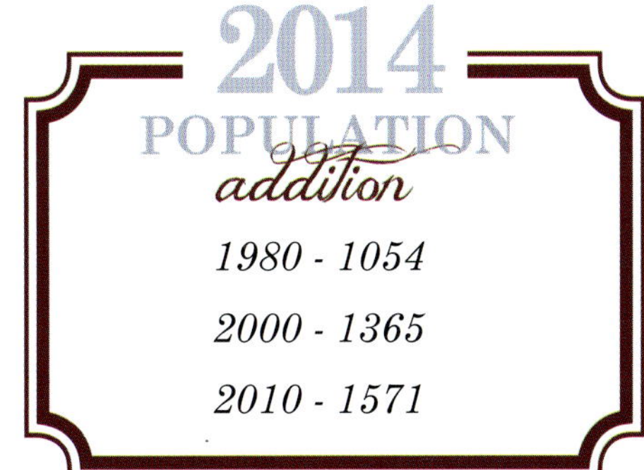

INTRODUCING THE LAKE MEADE COMMUNITY

Lake Meade residents congratulate the East Berlin Community for reaching a historic milestone, the 250th Anniversary of the founding of the town. Despite moderate growth and inevitable change, the historic core of East Berlin continues to illustrate the streets, lot layouts, and many fine examples of early architecture of a late 18th century town settled by German and Swiss immigrants. While the population has diversified, the community and its surroundings still retain aspects of lifestyle and landscape associated with rural settings in Germany. Lake Meade residents appreciate the quaintness, friendliness, and services of all kinds that our neighbor, East Berlin, has to offer.

According to the 2010 Census, Lake Meade had a population of 2,563 permanent residents. In addition, several hundred people own "second homes" or recreational lots at Lake Meade. Many of them spend numerous weekends enjoying the facilities and the ambience of the surrounding communities. In 1964, when East Berlin celebrated its Bicentennial Anniversary, Lake Meade did not exist! However, nearby Mud Run Valley, that lies between Germany and Stoney Point Roads, contained about a dozen farms and several smaller properties that were purchased in 1965 by the American Realty Service Corporation. A majority of the acreage was located in Reading Township, and a smaller portion was located in Latimore Township. East Berlin is a ten minute drive from the Lake Meade Community.

Back then, American Realty was the oldest and largest developer of "inland lake communities" in America. The developer purchased the land without government assistance and began to design a Master Plan for a community of approximately 1,400 individual lots, various common areas, and a 291-acre man-made lake.

To accomplish this, the company had to construct an earthen dam, which is 1,450 feet long and which has an adjoining concrete spillway 175 feet in width. By Memorial Day weekend of 1968, the lake was filled with water.

Due to the proximity of the proposed lake to the Civil War Battle Field of Gettysburg, the impoundment was named Lake Meade after General George G. Meade, the commanding officer of the Gettysburg Battle. The individual streets were named for senior officers of both armies and the presiding Presidents at that time. The Master Plan called for a privately constructed and maintained road system with 18 miles of paved cartways. One collector road, which extends for 5.5 miles, completely encircles the lake. Other attributes of the Master Plan included ten waterfront recreational areas, which provide docks, fishing access, and picnic facilities for residents who do not own a lakeside lot. The design also includes a stormwater management system that is quite different from the curbed streets and inlets found in typical suburban subdivisions. Instead, American Realty designed a street system that employed "contour grading" to enhance infiltration and reduce "ponding" on roadways. Finally, Lake Meade was initially provided with a central water system. Years later a public sewer system was installed.

In the beginning, American Realty conceived Lake Meade as a "perfect location for second homes designed for stress relief and family fun." Initial marketing campaigns focused on South Central and Northern Maryland. The developers recognized the importance of nearby East Berlin, and they placed a high value on the surrounding Pennsylvania German influenced rural landscapes and culture. In 1967, the Company held a promotional carnival at the site that featured a merry go round and the Buddy Rich Band. Attendance prizes included "two automatic shotguns just in time for hunting season."

Soon thereafter, a promotional brochure touting Lake Meade's location in the "heart of Pennsylvania Dutch Country" was produced. In addition to beautiful Pennsylvania German (Dutch) folkart designs, the brochure even included various phrases in original Pennsylvania German dialect.

Potential lot purchasers were admonished to "sagen good bye ihr aernschte sache." In English, this means "say goodbye to life's heavy things." The brochure also suggested to buyers that "Alle Gute Ding Drei" which means "All good things come in threes." American Realty then promoted advantages for "Recreation, Retirement, and Sound Investment" at Lake Meade. This approach must have worked because the lots sold quickly.

By 1968 sufficient lots sold so that it became necessary to form the "Lake Meade Property Owners Association", which is governed by an elected, but unpaid, Board of Directors, who are supported by an array of volunteer-based standing committees and community organizations. The need for volunteers to participate in governance and community affairs has been evident at Lake Meade since its inception.

The Lake Meade Community has grown enormously since the late 1960s, and many adjustments and enhancements have been made. By 2014, a total of 1,068 houses have been built. In the early days, 80 percent of all homes were used for second "vacation homes." Only 20 percent were occupied year round. This mix has now completely reversed; 80 percent of the existing homes are occupied on a permanent basis. The community remains attractive to all age groups.

Architectural styles and purchase price points vary substantially. The following are examples of a few of the enhancements that were necessary to meet the needs of a growing community:

LAKE MEADE TIMELINE

- **Lake Meade Municipal Authority formed (1969)**
- **Lake Meade Fire and Rescue Inc. formed (1975)**
- **Homemakers Club formed (1976)**
- **Sewer plant completed (1977)**
- **LMMA purchased water system from American Utilities (1983)**
- **Pyrotechnic Society (fireworks) formed (1988)**
- **Fire Company expands facilities (1995)**
- **Rehab of Swimming Pool and Community Center (1997 and 2000)**

These enhancements occurred through efforts of volunteer board members, committee members, and residents. One of the most significant committee recommendations was made in 1991 by the Finance Committee. As a result, Lake Meade began to track major infrastructure needs as well as to project income and expenses, and "pay as-you-go" principles were instituted. This way Lake Meade was able to construct a maintenance building, improve the sports complex and many of the lakeside dock facilities. One bridge has been replaced and roads have been improved. No special assessments or loans have been necessary.

By 2014, Lake Meade has emerged as a large residential community just outside of East Berlin. Much of the beautiful farmland separating the Lake from the Borough of East Berlin has been preserved. At the same time, we share schools, churches, business services, a library, a regional community center and a post office. The Lake Community continues to evolve. While volunteerism remains essential, the Lake now relies on a professional staff for administrative support, grounds maintenance, and safety. New committee activities have resulted in website development. Traditional activities such as scouting, garden club, homemakers and many others remain popular, as new activities emerge to meet community needs.

Richard Schmoyer,

Member of the Lake Meade Communications Committee

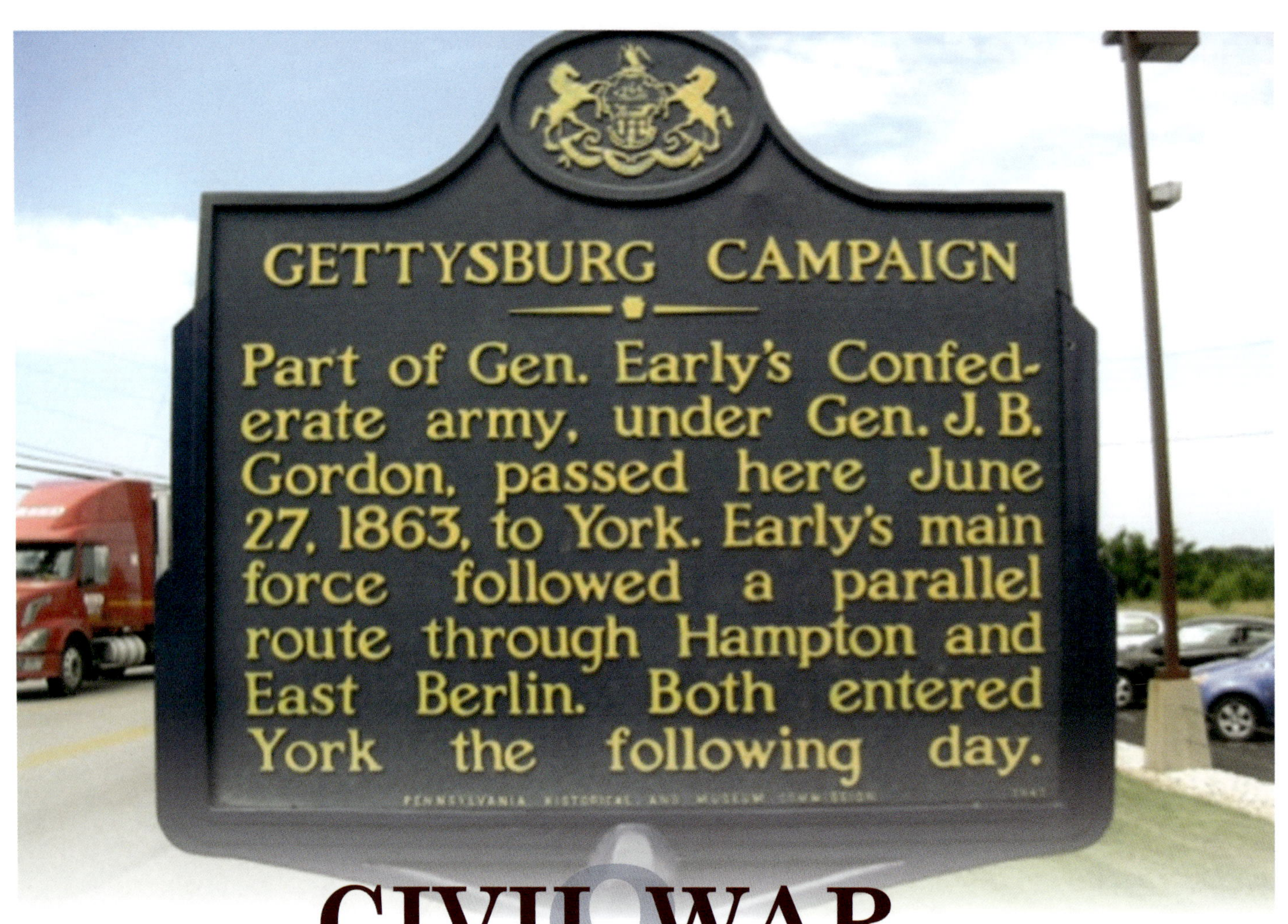

CIVIL WAR & EAST BERLIN

In the past 50 years, we have learned more about the Civil War, otherwise known as the Northern Aggression, and its effect on East Berlin. In 1964, during the bicentennial, very little was known as to how well East Berlin faired during this era. Today with research through books, letters, newspapers and diaries from that time period, more information has come to light. And of course we cannot forget the internet when it comes to obtaining information on any topic.

GENERAL JUBAL EARLY

News of the war broke on April 18, 1861, in York County and Adams County, with a story about the bombardment and surrender of Fort Sumter in the York County Star and Wrightsville Advertiser. The war didn't physically make its presence known to the area until June of 1863 when General Jubal Early and his 2nd Corps marched not once but twice through East Berlin. After the death of Thomas J. "Stonewall" Jackson to friendly fire on his way to the Battle of Chancellorsville in Virginia, General Robert E. Lee split his 20,000 plus man 2nd Corp into three divisions and placed them under General Jubal Early, General Edward Johnson and General Robert Rhodes. General Early was a 46-year-old U.S Military Academy graduate and a Virginia lawyer with a cantankerous personality. General Lee called General Early "My bad old man" but valued his tenacity. Gen. Early's division was organized into four brigades and further broken down into 17 regiments. At the start of the war, a regiment consisted of 1,000 men; but by 1863, due to casualties, it became less than half that size.

On June 27, 1863, General Early started his march east from Mummasburg to pass through Hunterstown, New Chester, and Hampton towards East Berlin. He planned to advance on to York then on to capture Harrisburg and perhaps even Philadelphia. That evening, Jubal Early looked for a place to spend the night among the farms a few miles to the east of East Berlin. He chose a large stone farmhouse owned by Mrs. Zinn in the small village of Big Mount. General Early wrote that he "firmly believed that the Confederate army would win; that we would soon dictate terms of peace in Philadelphia and New York and the war would then be over."

After settling in at the Zinn farmhouse with his staff, General Early rode to meet General John B. Gordon at the Jacob S. Altland's farm in Farmers to talk about what they could face when they rode into York. If they met no opposition from the Union forces, then General Gordon was to proceed onto Wrightsville and secure the bridge on both ends. On Sunday, June 28, 1863 General Gordon's troops marched through York towards Wrightsville by what is now known as Route 30, whereas General Early marched on the Canal Road into Weiglestown and then into York, Pa. When the Confederates arrived in York, General Early demanded of the chief Burgess (Mayor) David Small the sum of $100,000.00, saying that, "In such a rich country as this, these people must have laid by immense sums. I am sure you can find it hoarded up in the farmer's canvas bags and housewives' stockings." He explained that he had thousands of men to provide for, and greenbacks, unlike the confederate money, had value. The townspeople could only fulfill $28,600.00 of the demand in cash but supplied other goods such as flour and clothing.

General Gordon marched into Wrightsville on Sunday evening and met with resistance from the Union troops commanded by Jacob Frick and Granville Haller. On orders from General Darius Couch, the two Union commanders were to destroy the bridge upon withdrawal from Wrightsville. The wooden bridge about 1¼ miles long and built to accommodate great stress, was made up of 28 spans and sat about 15 feet above the Susquehanna

River. Robert Crane, a Wrightsville native, led a team of 19 carpenters to work on separating the roof and sides of fourth span from the west bank. Then holes were drilled and powder charges inserted in the arches and fuses were attached. At 7:30 p.m. the order was issued to blast the bridge. The charges were set off, the blast rocked the structure, but the span did not fall. Frick, commanding the rear of the retreat and seeing the bridge did not fall ordered his men to burn it. The bridge, which had already been soaked in kerosene and crude oil in hopes that the blast would start a fire, was easily ignited.

Jubal Early headed for Wrightsville on Sunday evening but when he saw the smoke from the burning bridge, he knew he would never march to Lancaster and then onto Harrisburg. Early conferred with Gordon and returned to York that night.

On Tuesday, June 30th, Generals John B. Gordon and Jubal Early left York and headed west. Early left around 7:00 a.m. with the rearguard and marched to Davidsburg. They proceeded along the road to East Berlin where the only incident that day came near the town. Lt. Colonel Elijah V. White, a Virginia horseman who served as chief scout for Gen Early, had a brush with a squad of federal horseman. White and his men earned the name "Comanches" for their piercing war cries when entering a battle. Early rode onto Dick Ewell's Headquarters in Heidlersburg where he received new orders from a messenger from Gen. Robert E. Lee. Ewell and Early's men would march east towards either Cashtown or Gettysburg and meet the rest of the Rebel forces.

STORIES *of* LOCAL INTEREST

Over the years there have been a few stories told about events that happened in East Berlin during the Civil War when Gen. Early marched through the town. Many of the residents were harassed by foraging patrols that were searching for food, clothing, fresh horses and mules. Here are a few of the stories. In some cases, residents, who were afraid of the consequences if they didn't comply, set out milk and bread for passing soldiers in hope of appeasing them. In other cases the people fled with their horses and livestock.

412 W. KING ST is known as the John & Catherin Fox Stone House, which was built in 1790, had communal bake ovens in the rear of the property. The women of the town would get together to bake the bread dough and socialize. Perhaps they gossiped about the latest events of the day, who had their clothes out on the line the earliest or who just had a baby in the area. But when the Rebels came through town on June 27th, 1863 the Confederate soldiers forced the women of the town to bake bread for them. While just a few houses east, the apothecary's house was being searched and liberated of its medicinal alcohol that the Apothecary kept in his basement.

EISENHART MILL is an old stone mill that sits just north of East Berlin on Eisenhart Mill Road. It was constructed around 1749 and was in use during the Civil War through the 1960's. It is a 3.5 story field stone and wood frame building. The Confederate troops, on their way to York and then onto Wrightsville, were raiding farms along the way for food and other necessities. They stopped at the mill and filled their supply wagons with barrels of freshly ground flour as well as corn, oats, and grain that had not yet been ground into flour.

There was a recorded incident near East Berlin on Early's return trip, where Lt. Colonel Elijah V. White and his Comanches scouts encountered a squad of federal horsemen. Could it have been near the old mill?

TAVERN TALES

There is told a tale of the house at **414 W. KING ST.** as being a tavern at the time of the Civil War and supposedly someone took a shot at a Confederate soldier from the second story window.

HAMON HOUSE

The house was built in 1892 by George and Charlotte Spangler. George was a merchant in Gettysburg. The house was built as a double so that a sister could live in the other half. Jeff and Raeann Hamon restored the home and received a preservation award from the Gettysburg Adams Historical Preservation Society.

426 WEST KING ST.

has been a tavern known as the Indian Queen or the Sign of the Indian Queen according to tavern license applications traced for a decade or more before 1814. Adam Swartz was granted a license renewed annually through 1825. His estate listed two lots of ground, lots 31 and 32, on which are a two-story dwelling house, part stone and part log -weather-boarded, with a one story back building, stabling, sheds and two wells of water. This property has been occupied as a tavern for a "great number of years."

It was sold to Thaddeus Stevens, a deed given on April 1, 1832. He was a State senator and advocate of abolition. When Stevens relocated to Lancaster in 1848, he sold the Swartz property to John Hartley. John Hartley (1820-1889) was a grandson of John Hildebrand, the proprietor of Berlin in 1794. Hartley and his wife Justine (1824-1902) spent fifty years of their lives together on this property and raised a large family.

Harold and Leslie Deardorff bought this property in 2006 and started renovations of the backyard. During the renovations three tombstones were found, two red shale stones for infants of the Hartley family, Edward and Joseph. The other white granite stone has the initials JB only. They are stored for safe-keeping.

Since the Union Cemetery was operating at that time and the Hartley family is buried there, the question is: are there graves of the children on this property in order to be close to their mother or were these red clay stones temporary ones?

MRS. ZINN'S FARMHOUSE

is located in the center of Big Mount which lies west of East Berlin. General Early spent the night of June 27th at the old farmhouse and had supper prepared for him by Mrs. Zinn and her daughter. Gen. Early noted that he "enjoyed a fare of 15 to 20 Pennsylvania German dishes," particularly fresh vegetables. He also noted that Mrs. Zinn used "earthy" language and that he noticed that her daughter did not blush during their conversation, so she must had been accustomed to such language. He concluded that he preferred the gentile manners of the Southern women to the coarse mouths of the women north of the Mason-Dixon Line.

LINCOLN...

There is also a story that the Confederates had threatened to kill anyone named "Lincoln," and it was rumored that there were two families in Dover who had boys with that name. The boys left Dover and hid in East Berlin until the Confederates had left the area.

GEORGE FROST KENNAN 1904-2005

Credit: Grace Warnecke

An influential American diplomat, a "Pulitzer-Prize" winning author and this country's elder statesman living in our midst.

In 1925 as a young man, George Kennan entered the Foreign Service and became an expert on Russia. After serving several years in Eastern European countries, he helped set up the new embassy in Moscow. When World War II commenced, Mr. Kennan was left in charge of the U.S. Embassy in Berlin Germany and was sesquestered by the Nazis along with his staff. In six months, an exchange was made, and this is when he decided to establish a home somewhere between New York and Washington, D.C. He was married to Annelise and had two children, Grace and Joan. In 1942, he found his farm near East Berlin. Mr. Kennan spent the remaining war years serving in Lisbon, London, and Moscow.

One of Kennan's dispatches from Moscow became known as the "Long Telegram" which became this country's grand strategy of containment guiding us through the "Cold War".

In 1951, Mr. Kennan was called back to active duty and became the Ambassador to Russia but was later asked to leave by Stalin.

In the mid 1950's Mr. Kennan returned from active duty with the State Department and accepted a chair at the Institute For Advanced Studies At Princeton to resume his scholarly pursuits. While there he wrote over 20 books and remained our country's leading expert on Russia. In 1961 President Kennedy appointed him Ambassador to Yugoslavia.

Over the 70 years of Kennan ownership, the farm in East Berlin has been a refuge for not only the Kennan family and their friends. In 1970, after Stalin's daughter defected from Russia, she spent the first summer in her new country at the farm where she burned her Russian passport in the barbeque [as she relates in her memoirs].

In 1982, he presented a paper to the American Philosophical Society in Philadelphia about East Berlin, PA. He said, "the people of the village have some particular qualities which I like to think of as outstandingly. If not uniquely those of small town and rural America, as I knew it in my childhood and still know it today: a certain kindness and helpfulness, a certain shrewdness tempered with modesty and a lively sense of humor and above all, a certain inner dignity."

George Kennan passed away in 2005 at the age of 101 years old.

Kennan en route to Moscow in May 1952

Joan F. Kennan Collection

Most recent books about GEORGE KENNAN:

George F. Kennan - An American Life - John Louis Gaddes

The Kennan Diaries - edited by Frank Costigliola

The Hawk and the Dove - Nicholas Thompson

Ambassador George Kennan is welcomed by Isabell & Robert Lau in front of the Studebaker House. The photo originally appeared in the York Sunday News.

Message to the East Berlin Bicentennial

Read by Joan Kennan (George Kennan's daughter) at the Bicentennial of 1964

I should like first to express my great regret that I cannot be present personally at the East Berlin Bicentennial. I and the members of my family are deeply attached to this town, not only because of the friendship and courtesy it has shown us as relative newcomers to the local community, but also because we have found so much to respect in its life and its people.

Beyond this there is something I would like to say about the Bicentennial itself. One of my deepest beliefs is that our lives can have no meaning if we think only of what they can give to us, the present generation, and fail to think of them as part of the past and part of the future. The world was not made for this generation alone. If we try to live just for ourselves, forgetting all that our forefathers have done for us and not caring what becomes of the world after our death, then I think we are letting down both our ancestors and our children, and it would be better if we had not lived at all. If we are to do God's work, in the sense of trying to make life more decent, more dignified and more hopeful in this country and in this world, we can do it only in a spirit of collaboration with our fathers and grandfathers on the one hand, and with our children and grandchildren on the other.

This is why I think it is such a fine thing that the Borough of East Berlin has set aside this week to refresh the memory of its own past, and by doing so, to honor the people who have struggled over two centuries, to make its life what it is today. This is in fact the finest sort of service East Berlin could render to the nation as a whole, because the selfishness and thoughtlessness and cynicism by which our American life is now so seriously affected are things that can be cured only at the local level: In the community, in the family, in the individual. If more communities could be brought to acknowledge a sense of obligation towards their own history this would be a better country. But, more important still, to recall the History of this town-to remember all the toil and faith and the suffering that have entered into the process of its life over the course of these two centuries, and to honor the people who bore all this on their shoulders-is simply another way of meeting the requirements of the very fundamental fifth commandment which was to "Honor thy Father and thy Mother."

My family and I are proud to be close neighbors of this town and to think of ourselves as members of its community. We congratulate it on the completion of these first two hundred years of its life-We wish it many more centuries of useful service--service to itself, to the world that surrounds it, and to the God in whose presence its citizens have always walked.

George Kennan

Typed from the original script June 9, 2014

The Night the World Came to an End

Excerpted from the book "*From the Highway to the Heavens*" (2013) by Jerry Mummert

Friday, July 7, 1952 was a typical hot, humid day. As evening closed in on the town, people came out of their houses to sit on the porches, drink iced tea or lemonade, and socialize with their neighbors and with the townsfolk who were out for a walk as the atmosphere became a bit more tolerable. The gang of teenagers with the fast cars had already gathered at Shetter's restaurant near the square on West King Street, "Dutch" Wagner (uncle to the Cashman boys) had already been to Lau's Variety Store for his Bromoseltzer with lemon, and Margaret Moul was patrolling the streets, looking for her cat. The mosquitos were rampant.

As evening turned into night into late night, people went to bed, hoping to find some way to get to sleep in spite of the humidity and the sweat - nobody had air-conditioning at that time.

At 2:15 a.m. the next morning, the town was jolted from sleep by an explosion followed by a loud, sustained roar. Looking out our north-facing windows, we saw that the sky was brilliant orange-red with flames leaping 200-300 feet into the air! "Area residents thought the blast was everything from thunder to an atomic bomb and the moon colliding with the earth. Roosters began crowing, chickens strutted about and birds started to sing in the trees." Fire sirens went off all over the area from York Springs to Dover. People in York and Lancaster Counties could see the sulphurous sky. I thought the world was coming to an end!

Several terrifying hours went by before we learned that the "Little Inch" natural gas pipeline had exploded about three miles north of town, along the Davidsburg Road, near Red Run Church, about 1,000 feet east of Route 194. By 5:30 a.m. the flames were extinguished when safety valves were closed at Marietta, Chambersburg, and Five Points (a few miles west of East Berlin along Route 234). The explosion and fire occurred on the farm of Mr. and Mrs. Edward Stieg, where three acres of oats were scorched and a swamp was dried up by the heat. "No appreciable damage resulted and no one was hurt."

The pipeline was originally constructed in 1943 of sub-standard war material metal. Owned by the Texas Eastern Company, the "Little Inch" stretched from Texas to Eaglesville, Montgomery County, Pennsylvania. Friction from gas escaping from a weak section of pipe probably caused the problem. Texas Eastern spent most of the next year checking out the remainder of the pipeline. Amazing enough, the same thing happened again even more dramatically in January, 1957!

Note: all quotes are from the York Gazette and Daily newspaper

Inch pipes stacked on a railroad, February 1943

Inch pipe, welding using roll-weld method

RELIGION

RELIGION

Union Church, which was located in the Union Cemetery plot, was constructed between 1811 and 1822. Lutheran and Reformed groups worshipped here. It was removed when these congregations built their own buildings. The Church School is pictured to the left of the Church; this building still stands at the southwestern edge of the Union Cemetery.

BERMUDIAN CHURCH OF THE BRETHREN

In 1849, the Big Conewago Congregation of the German Baptist Brethren was divided to form the Lower Conewago and the Upper Conewago Congregations. The Love Feasts of this congregation were held in the barn of the Casper Markey Farm near Mulberry until the first Bermudian meeting house was built in 1856. Services were held in the homes of C. T. Raffensperger at Mulberry and Daniel Trimmer near Kralltown.

In 1856, one lot was purchased from William Harlacher, Sr., and another from Peter Trimmer. These two tracts composed the plot on which the first Bermudian meeting house was built. At the same time, a small plot was laid out for a cemetery. The amount for the lots was $94.34¼ cents. Cost of the first meeting house amounted to $1500.

Due to the growth of the congregation, the Bermudian house became too small, especially during Love Feast occasions. As a result of this growth, the present building was erected in 1887. Since 1887, the Church building has been remodeled several times.

The present congregation consists of 189 members with the Reverend O. Wayne Cook as presiding elder.

EVANGELICAL CHURCH

The building pictured here once housed the congregation of the Evangelical Church. Later, the church was remodeled and enlarged to become the P.O.S. of A. Hall. Again at a later date, the building was remodeled and converted into a house now occupied by Borough Secretary, Curtis Eisenhart.

KRALLTOWN EVANGELICAL AND MENNONITE CHURCH

This Church was built in 1888 by members living in the community who found that the distance to other churches was too great for family travel.

The first Evangelical minister was A. Longsdorf. The first Sunday School Superintendent was Daniel Croul.

Sunday School was held each Sunday. Each congregation had its services on alternate Sundays.

In 1950, the Mennonites bought the entire Church. Harold Housman was the first Mennonite Sunday School Superintendent.

The present minister is the Reverend John C. Roher. At present, the Sunday School Superintendent is Leander Gantz; his assistant is Kraybill Miller.

LOWER BERMUDIAN LUTHERAN CHURCH

The Lower Bermudian Lutheran Church is one of the oldest churches in Adams County. The history of this Church dates back to 1745. At that time, the first Union Church was established by a group of German-speaking people of the Lutheran and Reformed Churches.

Meetings were held in the house of Johannes Aspers and in other dwellings until 1745, when it was resolved to accept the offer of Jacob Heens, Reformed, of two acres of land for a Union Reformed and Lutheran Church so that the clear and unadulterated Word of God could be preached and the Holy Sacraments devoutly administered. The Church was consecrated on April 15, 1754 by Pastor Bacher for the Lutherans and Jacob Lischy of the Reformed Church.

The first church was a plain, log cabin characteristic of the period, and was familiarly known as "Longgreen." From 1754, a book was kept containing regular entries of ministerial acts verifying the great pastoral care of the early days.

In these early years, the Lutheran Church in America had few ordained ministers; and those available had to serve congregations spread over a large area. It is known that the Reverend George Bacher had some relationship to the Lower Bermudian Congregation and that the Reverend Jacob Goering received by confirmation a class of twenty-three boys and twenty-four girls on Easter, 1777. A church had been established at Abbottstown, and its pastors also visited this church.

On March 2, 1795 formal plans were made for a new building. The building was to be built of stone and lime; eighteen feet in front and thirty-eight feet in length and thirty-five feet in breadth were to be the dimensions of the proposed structure. The work was done by Valentine Fickes. As before, this was a Union Church and was sometimes referred to as Zion's, though this name was not adopted officially.

The building was repaired and renovated in 1820. The Reverend J. J. Albert was the Lutheran pastor at that time.

In 1871, the Reformed congregation sold its interest in the building and lot to the Lutherans; and on May 19, a corner stone was laid at a new brick building known as Mt. Olivet on the opposite side of the road. Several years later, the Lutherans razed their old building and erected a brick building; this was dedicated December 6, 1879. This is the building which is used for worship at the present time.

During the remainder of the nineteenth century and part of the twentieth century, the Word of God was preached and the Sacraments administered in the Church by a number of faithful pastors.

Beginning in 1950, several significant improvements were made on both the sanctuary and the basement. The Church was re-dedicated after being completely repainted on the inside and after the installation of the new heating system. A number of other improvements were made on the building, all of which took place during the pastorate of the Reverend Norman Bortner, who served the congregation from 1950 to 1960.

For a number of years, the Lower Bermudian Lutheran Church formed one parish with the York Springs Lutheran Church and the Chestnut Grove Lutheran Church, which is located near York Springs. In 1960, the York Springs Lutheran Church began a separate ministry; the Lower Bermudian and Chestnut Grove Churches remained to comprise the Latimore Lutheran Parish.

In June, 1963 this parish extended a call to the Reverend M. Benson Paull, who is serving the parish at the present time.

METHODIST EPISCOPAL CHURCH

The earliest entry in the records of the York Springs Methodist Circuit pertaining to the East Berlin Methodist Episcopal Church was dated in 1884. Apparently, the Church was in existence prior to that time; but no information could be lotated concerning events prior to the date aforementioned.

On December 24, 1844 the following persons were elected trustees of the East Berlin Methodist Episcopal Church at the quarterly conference held at New Oxford: John Barnitz, Levi Chronister, Jacob Peters, Wesley Sadler, J. Edward Herman, Issac Sadler, Amos Bender and John Tudor. The York Springs Circuit included: Rock Chapel, Petersburg (York Springs), Hanover, Oxford (New Oxford), Hunterstown, Hampton, Bendersville, Wenksville, Pine Grove, Sowers Schoolhouse, Berlin (East Berlin), and Spring Forge.

The quarterly meeting of the churches of the circuit was held at Berlin on May 15, 1852.

It was reported to the second quarterly meeting on August 6, 1853 that the Sunday School at Berlin was inactive. A subscription was taken for the benefit of the Berlin Sunday School amounting to $6.50.

On October 18, 1853 the quarterly conference reported that the Berlin Sunday School had been reactivated and doing nicely. There were 6 officers, 30 scholars and an average attendance of 20.

The Board of Trustees of the East Berlin Methodist Episcopal Church asked the quarterly conference held on December 30, 1865 for permission to sell the church premises. It was agreed that the request should be granted and that the proceeds of the sale should be applied to the rebuilding of the church at Petersburg (York Springs). John Tudor, John Pfleiger, J. E. Herman, Jacob Peters and A. B. Dell were the trustees.

The trustees were authorized to sell the church building on May 11, 1873. There is no further mention of this transaction or of the future of the Methodist congregation in the minutes of the York Springs Methodist Circuit.

MORNING HOUR CHAPEL

On an old United States Geographic Survey Map of the area of Reading Township and about three and one-half miles from East Berlin, a settlement consisting of a milk station, a store and several houses is designated as Amatus. At one time, a small schoolhouse was located along this same road which was known as *Germany* prior to World War I, after which the name was changed to *Victory*.

This schoolhouse was in an area surrounded by churches but none of these were within the immediate proximity of the residents of this community. Since transportation was not satisfactory, many homes neglected public worship. Unfortunately, the children roamed about the community with no place to go on Sunday mornings. Mervin Bosserman, then a small boy, suggested that the Reverend Elias Leatherman, a member of the township school board, be consulted concerning the use of *Victory* for Sunday School purposes. Consent was given; and on September 14, 1930, a Sunday School was opened. The name *Morning Hour* was chosen because the Sunday School convened at nine a.m.

Mary A. Stoner was the first teacher; fourteen pupils were present at the first service. Attendance during the first year averaged sixteen, and offerings averaged fifty-nine cents.

On the first Rally Day, September 12, 1931, an adult class was formed. This group was taught by the Reverend S. B. Stoner until three months before his death in 1958. Sometimes a brief worship was connected with the Sunday School session. Later, regular morning worship services followed the Sunday School period.

In 1960, the schoolhouse was sold and purchased by the *Morning Hour* group and incorporated under the Brethren in Christ Church. A denominational organization was formed with twenty-three charter members.

Since the capacity of the building was inadequate for all those who wished to worship, a decision was reached that a small church be erected adjacent to the schoolhouse on land donated by Joseph A. Stoner. Ground was broken in April, 1962; the new building was dedicated on January 12, 1963. The average Sunday School attendance for the first half of 1963 was eighty-eight. The present Church membership is twenty-seven. The Reverend Victor E. Nichols, a senior at Messiah College of Grantham serves as the part-time pastor. Joseph A. Stoner is the deacon, and Ronald K. Stoner is Sunday School Superintendent. Benny Fadenrecht is lay minister and assistant superintendent of the Sunday School.

MOUNT OLIVET UNITED CHURCH OF CHRIST

The Mount Olivet United Church of Christ had its beginning in 1745 when the Evangelical Lutheran and Reformed people met at the home of Henrich Weiden Bach (Weidenback) to consider the organization of a Christian Church. For nine years, these people held worship in homes and barns of its members.

On April 14, 1754 a log church was dedicated on land given by Jacob Heen, Reformed. In 1797, the log church was replaced by a stone church which was used by both Lutheran and Reformed Churches until 1871. In that year, the Reformed congregation sold its rights to the Lutheran congregation and built a brick church across the road.

In 1934, Mount Olivet joined in a church union to form the Evangelical and Reformed Church and in 1957 in a larger union to form the United Church of Christ.

The first pastor to serve the church was Jacob Lischy in 1754. The present pastor is Ernest W. Brindle, who began his services in 1959.

PARADISE PROTECTORY

Immaculate Heart of Mary Parish goes back to the earliest days of Catholicity in York County. Its boundaries are intimately associated with the historic settlement founded by the Jesuit Fathers at Conewago Chapel in 1721.

The cornerstone of the present Parish Rectory bears the date of 1761; this is part of the original wall of the house built by Samuel Wise as his residence. Mass was offered here on several occasions.

One of the early settlers, Fredrick Brandt moved to the vicinity of Abbottstown (then Berwick) about 1800 and purchased 237 acres. In his will he donated the farm and land to the church. Early in 1810, he had a large stone home built. An upstairs room was used as a chapel until the present church was completed in 1845.

The construction of the church was under the supervision of a local contractor, but a great deal of the work was done by the parishioners themselves.

In 1860, Mary Dellone donated money for the two bells.

The Jesuit Fathers relinquished their spiritual direction of the parish in 1891.

During 1904, the first full-time resident pastor was appointed; under his direction, the present rectory was built.

The Parish was given into the hands of the Irish Capuchin Fathers in 1911. They directed the Brothers conducting the New Paradise Protectory and Agriculture School.

In 1931, the Capuchin Fathers returned the Parish to the Diocesean Priests.

During the year of 1949, the interior of the church was renovated; and a new stone bell tower was added. This work was accomplished by a generous gift from Mr. Heltzel.

The church has seen a steady growth from a few pioneers to the present six hundred parishioners.

PARADISE UNION CHURCH — HOLTZSCHWAMM

This historic Church located in Paradise Township, York County, was established in 1775. Much of the area was a woody swamp, or Holtzschwamm, a favorite resort of the Indians. The first church building was a log cabin erected in the center of the old graveyard. The first Lutheran minister was the Reverend Jacob Goehring, and the first Reformed minister was the Reverend William Vandersloot.

Through the years many additions and improvements were made on the buildings and grounds, including the following: the first bell was placed on June 19, 1880; new chandeliers and pulpit furniture were purchased in 1884; the iron fence was placed around the old graveyard in 1907; electric lights were installed in the old Church in 1925; the chancel and choir loft were built in the front part of the building in 1935; the orgatron was added in 1942; the interior of the old Church was repainted and decorated in 1943.

On November 7, 1954 a ground-breaking ceremony for the new Church was conducted. Those taking part were the oldest Lutheran member, Jacob Trostle, and the oldest Reformed member, Eli Gross.

The cornerstone was placed on March 27, 1955. Dedication services took place during the week of September 16, 1956.

The first ministers in the new Union Church were the Reverend George A. Clark, Lutheran, and the Reverend J. Keller Brantley, Reformed.

After about five years in the new Union Church at Holtzschwamm, it was recommended by both Synods that this Union be dissolved; this took place on February 1, 1963 at which time the Lutheran Congregation purchased the Reformed Congregation's share. The Reformed Congregation purchased a fifteen-acre tract of land on the north side of the Lincoln Highway and east of Farmers where they expect to erect a new Church and Church School.

The present Lutheran pastor is the Reverend Jack E. Herrera; the Reformed pastor is the Reverend Charles E. Strasbaugh.

RED MOUNT CHURCH

The (Bermudian Bower) Red Mount Evangelical Church had its beginning in a schoolhouse which was built in 1827 at a cost of $138.75. This building was presented to the community as a place of education and religious meetings. Beginning in 1829, the worship period was conducted by the followers of Jacob Albright, who founded the Evangelical Church in Eastern Pennsylvania.

The present Church is the third building. A stone building erected in 1853 was dismantled and some of the stones were used for the foundation of the present building, which was constructed in 1888.

The first elected Sunday School Superintendent was G. W. Detter; the present Superintendent is Ralph Sealover.

The first Conference Pastor was A. Longsdorff in 1868; the present pastor is Warren W. Costic.

ST. PAUL'S CHURCH — RED RUN

Saint Paul's Lutheran and Reformed Church, commonly known as Red Run, is located along the York and Shippensburg Road in Washington Township, York County, about thirteen miles northwest of York.

The history of the Church, which was long known as Sowers Church, began on July 4, 1843, when George Sours, Sr. (commonly spelled Sowers) and his wife Elizabeth, by their deed, conveyed to George Sours, Jr., John W. Smith and John Shive, a tract of land for the erection of a house of worship for the sum of one silver dollar, lawful money of the United States of America.

No record can be located concerning the organization of a church prior to the laying of the cornerstone for the building on April 21, 1844, when the services were conducted by the Reverend Peter Sheurer and the Reverend John E. Albert. In connection with the laying of the cornerstone, the following was adopted:

"DECLARATION

"Since it has been inconvenient in this neighborhood to attend divine services, since we live distant from all surrounding churches, THEREFORE, we have in the name of our great God, and our Lord Jesus Christ, organized, and have resolved to build a house in which we and our children can gather together to worship our God, and to be upbuilded through the preaching of His word in our holy faith.

"This church, which shall be known as Saint Paul's Church, will be built in Washington Township, in the county of York, in the State of Pennsylvania, in the sixty-eighth (68th) year of the Independence of the United States, under the reign of President John Tyler, and Governor David R. Porter of Pennsylvania. This church shall forever be an evangelical protestant church, in which the Evangelical Lutheran and the High German Reformed shall hold their services. In this church shall be taught no other doctrine but that corresponding with the Augsburg Confession and the Heidelberg Catechism.

"For the future of our children, and our children's children, and all those coming after us, we herewith lay in this cornerstone one Bible and two catechisms, one Lutheran and one Reformed.

"This done this 21st day of April in the year of our Lord, one thousand eight hundred and forty-four. Pastors present: Peter Sheurer and John E. Albert. Building Committee: John W. Smith, George Sours and John Shive."

The first baptism recorded was that of Lena Ann, daughter of Charles and Magdalena Swartz, born June 24, 1844, baptized October 6, 1844.

The congregations have worshipped in union and in the spirit of Christian fellowship ever since in the same building, which remains in splendid preservation. The present ministers are the Reverend Charles A. Snyder and the Reverend William H. Anderman, Jr., Pastor Snyder serves as the Lutheran minister while Pastor Anderman serves as the United Church of Christ minister.

Remodeling and enlargements to the original church were made on four occasions, and dedication services were held as follows: June 1 and 2, 1912; November 22-29, 1927; May 2, 1954 and April 9-16, 1961.

TRINITY LUTHERAN CHURCH

The first known effort to build a church in East Berlin was in 1811, when Lutheran and German Reformed members began soliciting funds from *all pious and Charitable Christians of any denominations.*

Records show that the building was not fully completed under terms of the first contract dated May 13, 1811. On July 26, 1822, the second contract was drawn up and the building was finished several months later.

Union preaching was done by anonymous supply pastors until the Reverend John Speck began his pastorate in the unfinished building on July 9, 1819. The Union Church building, which stood due east of the present cement walk through the cemetery, was later razed by the Reformed Congregation; and many of the materials were used in the erection of the present Zwingli Church.

The earliest record of efforts by the Lutherans to establish a separate place of worship occurred on October 22, 1886. The church council voted to build a two-story brick building in the Borough of East Berlin.

On October 22, 1887 J. R. Darone, local contractor, started to erect the building; it was finished November 19, 1888.

The Union Church served both congregations until May 11, 1889, when the Lutherans sold their interest for $250.

The new Church, Trinity Lutheran, was dedicated free of debt on May 26, 1889. The first minister was the Reverend John Tomlinson.

Trinity was one of a three-member parish until October 11, 1893, when New Oxford united with an organized Mission at McSherrystown, leaving East Berlin and Abbottstown to constitute a parish.

An annex, to be used as a Primary Sunday School Room was built by A. B. Trimmer, local contractor, and dedicated December 12, 1900.

In December 1909, the first pipe organ was installed at a cost of $2000, with $1250 donated by Andrew Carnegie.

Other improvements and additions to be effected during the period from 1920 to 1948 were: enlarging of the Primary Room, redecoration of the Church Nave, addition of the Junior Choir loft, and the conversion of the heating plant from coal to gas fuel.

In 1952, an annex was erected to be used as a multi-purpose room.

On May 27, 1956 the congregation purchased a lot at the rear of the Church for parking space.

On March 3, 1957 Trinity and St. John's congregations voted to dissolve the union that existed since October 11, 1893. After the vote was sanctioned by the Church Conference, Trinity became a separate self-supporting charge as of July 1, 1957.

On October 13, 1957 the congregation purchased a lot on East King Street for the erection of a parsonage. On September 28, 1958 the parsonage was dedicated.

On September 17, 1961 the congregation decided to install a new Moller Pipe Organ, chimes, tower music system and interior sound system. These improvements were used for the first time on December 9, 1962.

The present pastor is the Reverend Harold Stoudt. The current membership numbers 631 baptized adults and children, 501 confirmed adults and 418 communing members.

UPPER CONEWAGO CONGREGATION CHURCH OF THE BRETHREN

The Upper Conewago Congregation came into existence in the year 1849 as the result of a division of the territory (then belonging to the Big Conewago Congregation) into two searate congregations, known as Big Conewago and Upper Conewago. The first minister was Adam Long.

In the beginning, there were nine centers of activity: Latimore, Mountain, Bermudian, Conewago, East Berlin, West Berlin, Longneckers, Pigeon Hills and Seven Hundred.

After the two congregations were divided, Upper Conewago did not have a place to worship. It was necessary to hold their meetings and Love Feasts in the houses and barns of church members.

In 1851, a tract of land was purchased near East Berlin for the sum of $20 to be used as a site for a meeting house. In 1852, a small stone meeting house was built, located at the site of the present Mummert's Meeting House.

In 1856, a second house of worship was built in Latimore Township near York Springs. Today, it is known as Latimore Meeting House.

From 1860 to 1886, the church grew so rapidly in its membership that the Five Points' and Baker's schoolhouses were used to take care of all the members.

In 1874, two more meeting houses were built — one near Hampton and the Trostle Meeting House located about four miles northwest of York Springs.

HAMPTON MEETING HOUSE

In 1822, the stone church at Mummert's was replaced by a brick church. This was the first church to provide overnight accommodations for those who came a great distance. The second floor was used for Love Feast Service; meals were provided in the basement.

In 1899, a meeting house was built in East Berlin on Locust Street.

Upper Conewago built its last meeting house on a plot which was donated by John L. Bosserman and wife, located near Baker's Schoolhouse in Reading Township. This building was dedicated November 22, 1903. After this, services in the Baker Schoolhouse were discontinued.

The first Sunday School was organized in East Berlin, January 1, 1902.

In 1915, the sisters of this congregation organized a Ladies' Aid Society. This group raised funds for various projects, such as: furnishing a mothers' room in the East Berlin Church and a dormitory room at Elizabethtown College.

In 1918, the Upper Conewago Congregation and the Brethren Cemetery Association were granted a Charter by the Adams County Circuit Court of Appeals.

On August 27, 1939 the Trostle Meeting House was reopened.

In 1942, the stones from the old schoolhouse were used for the construction of a fence around the cemetery at Mummert's.

In 1956, the East Berlin House was remodeled to comply with the sewer regulations of the Borough.

Services at Hampton were discontinued in 1960, because the house no longer offered adequate space accommodations for the congregation.

The Congregation is supporting Brother and Sister Good on the mission field in Nigeria, Africa.

These ministers are serving this congregation at the present time: Ralph Schildt, Vernon Nell, Harry Nell, Dale King and Hershey Keller.

Recently, Mummert's Meeting House was remodeled to provide rest-room facilities and two Sunday School rooms.

ZWINGLI CHURCH

Before a church was built, the worship services were held in the homes of some of the worshipers, whenever a minister came through the community. According to our records, the first minister was the Reverend John Ernst from 1777 to 1804.

The first church building was erected on a site purchased October 5, 1811 from the estate of John and Margaret Hildebrand. This spot was located on the front portion of the Union Cemetery. Due to the many difficulties involved, the building was not completed until 1822. This first church was built by

the German Lutherans and German Reformed people.

In 1888, the Lutherans built their own church on West King Street. On June 15, 1890 the Reformed Congregation built their church on West King Street, where it remains today.

Several changes took place in the naming of the congregation. In the beginning, it was known as a "Union" Church; when the new building was completed, it was called *Zwingli*, named for the Swiss Reformer, Ulrich Zwingli.

At one time, Zwingli Church was one of a four-church parish, consisting of Zwingli, East Berlin, Emanuel, Hampton; Mt. Olivet; Bermudian and St. Paul's (Red Run). In 1915, St. John's of New Chester was added, making it a five-church charge served by one pastor.

In 1927, a two-manual, Moeller pipe organ was installed. In 1940, an addition was placed at the rear of the church providing room for Church School and social functions, as well as, a kitchen and rest rooms.

In 1949, the Board of National Missions decided to give help to the pastor by having student pastors from the Theological Seminary of Lancaster offer assistance. By so doing, each of the five churches had worship services each Sunday. The Reverend William H. Anderman, Jr. was the first student assistant.

In 1949 and 1950, the interior of the nave was completely remodeled by relocating the pulpit, communion table, pews, new chancel and organ console.

Stained glass windows were installed in the nave in 1957.

In 1957, a merger took place. The Evangelical and Reformed Church merged with the Congregational Christian Church into a body known as *The United Church of Christ*. It is under this name that the Congregation is serving today.

In 1959, the five-point charge was split into two separate charges. At this time, the new East Berlin Charge was composed of Zwingli, East Berlin, and St. Paul's Church (Red Run). The present pastor is the Reverend William H. Anderman, Jr.

TRINITY EVANGELICAL LUTHERAN CHURCH,

From 1964-2014

Established in 1811, is pleased to be a part of the East Berlin's long history and looks forward to the next 50 years of serving Christ and community! Composed of approximately 280 members today. Trinity offers a beautiful blend of old and new. Each week's Sunday worship includes Holy Communion, Christian education programs for all ages, and a variety of music including organ, piano, choir, and bell choir.

Trinity and its members have been actively involved in our local community for several decades through programs such as the Food Pantry and Colonial Days. Ministry has included the Trinity Prayer Chain, support to missionaries in India and Tanzania, support to camping ministry, and mission trips to disaster-affected areas in the U.S.

Since East Berlin's 200th anniversary, Trinity has also undergone several upgrades. The Moller pipe organ, first dedicated in 1963, was rebuilt in 1992. Renovations in 1986 and 1998 included modifications and improvements to the chapel, parlor, and nave, as well as the addition of several classrooms, social areas, a music room, elevator and ramp for wheelchair access. In 2009, the kitchen was completely renovated to support fellowship and fundraising events. Like its facilities, the people of Trinity are always being made new by the Holy Spirit, equipped to do God's work with our hands!

Located at 117 W. King St.
Worship at 9am each Sunday morning.
Sunday School at 10:30am

Pastor: Rev George Scott
Organist: Karen Wire

East Berlin, Pennsylvania

ZWINGLI UNITED CHURCH OF CHRIST

From 1964 - 2014

Zwingli United Church of Christ is located at 403 West King Street about two blocks west of the square in the Borough of East Berlin. The early history of the church is linked with Rev. John E. Ernst (1744-1804) as its founder. An itinerant minister from Lancaster County, Rev. Ernst is buried in the East Berlin Union Cemetery having succumbed to yellow fever which wiped out a large part of the Berlin population.

In 1959 Zwingli and St. Paul's (Red Run) became a two-point charge until 1966 when it was dissolved. In 1979, Zwingli called their first full-time pastor, Rev. Allen Heckman. That same year, the sanctuary was remodeled.

In the early 1980's, a large addition was added –a new social room, remodeled kitchen, and an educational wing. The property at 407 West King Street was purchased for the future parsonage. In 1981, Zwingli began a Mother's Morning Out program, which grew into a Nursery School for four-year old children. Over the next few years this ministry developed into Zwingli Christian School, which has provided a very successful ministry in Early Childhood Educational programs for pre-school, kindergarten, day-care children and their families.

Zwingli's ministry to others continues to grow. Food is collected weekly, drives are held throughout the year, and members serve to support the Abbottstown-East Berlin Food Bank. School supplies, clothing and monetary donations are made to missionaries who serve in Costa Rica. An outreach to serve the needy in the community is a year round mission. Hats, scarves, mittens and gloves have been collected every year for 12 years for the Adams County Holiday Outreach Bureau. Each year over a thousand warm items are donated to needy children by Zwingli members. Zwingli is always very generous with time and money whenever there is a need.

During Vacation Bible School, a hot meal is provided each evening to over 100 children from the surrounding community. AWANA has been very successful reaching out to many in the community. The facility also has become Red Cross-certified for emergencies. Zwingli's doors have always been open to many community organizations, providing a meeting place for their use. The Lions, TOPS, Girl Scouts and Boy Scouts, CROP Walk, and blood drives are some of many organizations who meet here. The MITE Society has provided many banquet meals, plus pie and soup sales over the years to help defray costs at Zwingli.

In September 2013, Zwingli's church tower was struck by lightning which caused many thousand dollars worth of damage to the equipment and the church facility. It also made the congregation realize the urgent need to make updates to the current facility.

Many areas are in need of repair along with some much-needed space. Several committees along with the church Consistory, are hoping to make changes and additions so our many programs can continue to grow in East Berlin and the surrounding community.

No matter where you are on your journey, you are always welcome to come to Zwingli United Church of Christ. Worship is at 9 a.m. each Sunday morning; Sunday School is at 10:15am.

Pastor: Rev. Dr. Margaret J. Wise

Organist: Mrs. Kay Guise

403 W. King St East Berlin, PA 17362

Telephone: 717.259.0623

www.zwingliucc.org

For East Berlin Founder's Day 250 Years

(May 8, 1764 to May 8, 2014)

A LITANY OF THANKS

On this great occasion of East Berlin Founder's Day 250 years ago, we are overwhelmed with gratitude for the blessings this town has received. We are thankful for those who have lived before us and those of us who live here now. We pray for those who will come after us. We are blessed! This week our gratitude pours out into our streets and alleys, back lanes and sidewalks, to reach up and out with gratitude towards so many and towards the One from whom all blessings flow. Alleluia and praise!

*-Thanks for the good green soil from which this town was carved---from land owned by the Richard and Thomas Penn and laid out by John Frankenberger, May 8th 1764.
We give thanks.*

*-For all forebearers of grace here in East Berlin---
those original farmers and builders and settlers--- our predecessors and parents. We give thanks.*

-For those who serve and have served the public welfare----postal workers, borough employees, keepers of records, financial officers and bank employees.

*-For those who make laws and regulations----for lawyers, borough council members and our mayor, Keith Hoffman.
We give thanks.*

-For those who keep us safe and free....the firefighters, rescue workers and EMT people of Liberty Fire Company #1 and police officers. We give thanks.

-For area organizations: the Historical Society, VFW, Lion's Club, Senior Citizens Center, The Free Mason's, Girl Scouts and Boy Scouts, Sport's clubs like Youth Baseball. We give thanks.

*-For places of education, past and present, including the old school house and our community center ---used in the past as a public school and now for community education---for preschools and day care centers and for our East Berlin Library.
We give thanks.*

-For parades, celebrations, for places of exercise and recreation---especially our new community park area. We give thanks.

-For all farmers, business owners and employees, factories and employees, landlords, renters and home owners. Passersby and all who in neighboring towns wish us well! We give thanks.

-For all those who heal and care for our health needs; all types of doctors, nurses, health aides, pharmacists, dentists. We give thanks.

For restaurant workers, groceries and gas suppliers and their employees, those who keep our computers working, those who maintain outdoor spaces, small shop keepers, including our well-known antique shops. We give thanks.

-For all places of worship, including our own homes and back yards. We give thanks.

-For the qualities that make this town great---cooperation, love of neighbor, fairness, tolerance, vigilance, security, courage to face hardships, integrity, long-range vision, welcome to strangers, truthfulness in all situations. We give thanks.

-For all the committees and workers who put together this celebration and those who will clean up afterward, for the choir, the re-enactors, parade marchers and organizers and all participants. We give thanks.

-And for all volunteers without whom this great town and great event today would be impossible. We give thanks!

-May we also follow the paths of goodness and peace for those who come after us; our children, grandchildren and beyond so that this town will prosper for new generations.

-May we go forth into these next days, weeks, and years thankful, hopeful and working together for the good of all!

- We bow in humble gratitude! Amen.

05/03/ 2014

EDUCATION

EDUCATION

Robert John Chester, an Englishman, opened the first English school in East Berlin in 1769. This experiment of an English school, at this early date in a German neighborhood, did not prove successful; and the self-sacrificing Englishman was soon obliged to give up the attempt as hopeless. He afterwards turned his attention to tavern keeping, which is said to have proved much more lucrative.

Apparently, from the sources of information available, there were church-operated schools in existence during the period 1769-1839. Data on these schools is rather fragmentary.

The Church School

In 1834, the Common School Law was enacted by the Pennsylvania General Assembly. Under the provisions of this law, the question of adoption or rejection of the common-school system was decided by the direct vote of the people of each voting district. Much opposition developed largely because of misapprehension and through ignorance of its provisions. A concerted movement for its repeal failed in the General Assembly in 1835 largely through the efforts of Governor Wolfe and the Honorable Thaddeus Stevens, who at that time was a member of the Legislature from Adams County. However, both men were defeated in their bids for re-election in 1836. Hamilton Township, of which East Berlin was a part, did not accept this law until 1839.

According to *A History and Directory of the Boroughs of Adams County,* published in 1880, the Berlin Improvement Society was founded in 1836 and occupied a school room owned by the Lutheran and Reformed Churches. It further states that this building was more than one hundred years old by 1880 and had a circulating library containing over six hundred volumes. This building, which still stands at the southwestern edge of the Union Cemetery, and a one-room brick building which stood at the western side of Harrisburg Street were the locations of the first public schools. Classes were held in the church-school building as recently as 1929.

The Select School, later known as the Normal School, in charge of Professor J. C. Hildebrand, was established in 1870 and was first held in the old public-school building.

This school gained a wide local reputation for thorough teaching. Scholars were attracted from near and far, many of whom were turned away because of lack of accommodations. *Grades A* and *B* were designed for teachers or those preparing to teach. *Grade C,* or the Model School, was designed for General Business Education.

J. Curtis Hildebrand, better known as *Master John,* became a legendary figure to numerous people in the community. There is no written record of his deeds and accomplishments, only the stories as told by one generation to the next remain with us. The *Hickory Stick* and *Razor Strap, so* often thought of in the early schools, were not determining factors in his disciplining. His personality and understanding, along with his giftedness in other fields as well as education, demanded the respect he received from his students and community. The dates of his birth and death still remain a secret, as told by his tombstone which stands in the Union Cemetery. This may indicate that *Master John's* philosophy was, *Only the deeds of man on earth determine his just reward.*

The East Berlin Select School had an annual catalogue which described its program offerings. The pages of one of these catalogues are reproduced on the pages to follow.

Master John

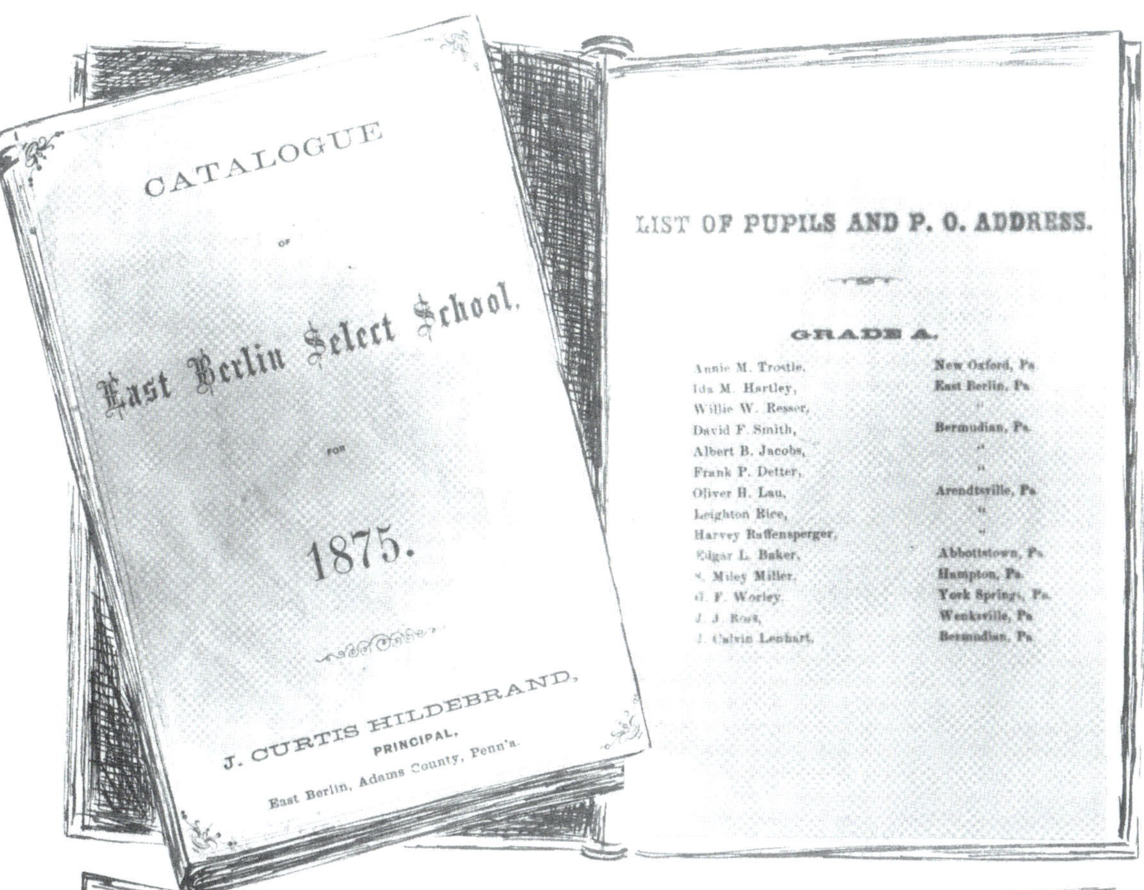

CATALOGUE

OF

East Berlin Select School,

FOR

1875.

J. CURTIS HILDEBRAND,

PRINCIPAL,

East Berlin, Adams County, Penn'a.

LIST OF PUPILS AND P. O. ADDRESS.

GRADE A.

Annie M. Trostle,	New Oxford, Pa
Ida M. Hartley,	East Berlin, Pa
Willie W. Resser,	"
David F. Smith,	Bermudian, Pa
Albert B. Jacobs,	"
Frank P. Detter,	"
Oliver H. Lau,	Arendtsville, Pa
Leighton Rice,	"
Harvey Raffensperger,	"
Edgar L. Baker,	Abbottstown, Pa
S. Miley Miller,	Hampton, Pa
G. F. Worley	York Springs, Pa
J. J. Ross,	Wenksville, Pa
J. Calvin Lenhart,	Bermudian, Pa

GRADE B.

Jennie King,	East Berlin, Pa.
Annie L. Spangler,	"
Katie L. Miller,	"
Katie Resser,	"
Lillie L. Wolf,	"
Maggie A. Chronister,	Hampton, Pa.
Louisa Hikes,	York Springs, Pa.
Lizzie Davis,	Abbottstown, Pa.
Isaac Miller,	"
Jas. B. Gladfelter,	"
Jeremiah W. Thoman,	"
Philip C. Milhr,	York Springs, Pa.
Jas. H. Gardner,	"
Eli Lerew,	"
J. Willie Tudor,	"
L. W. Lighty,	Mulberry, Pa.
Amos H. Heneise,	Big Mount, Pa.
Calvin L. Sebright,	East Berlin, Pa.
C. B. Kauffman,	"
Michael O. Maul,	"
Jas. B. Stoner,	"
Jas. W. Hartley,	"
Lewis L. King,	"
Allen Hartman,	"
Harry L. Myers,	New Oxford, Pa.
J. Ed. Britcher,	"
Willie E. Shelley,	Kralltown, Pa.
Jos. H. Hikes,	Round Hill, Pa.
Jas. C. Deardorff,	Hampton, Pa.
Frank J. Snyder,	New Chester, Pa.

GRADE C.

Emma J. Hartman,	East Berlin, Pa.
Emma J. Bushey,	"
Elmer L. Lewis,	"
Jno. H. Nitchman,	"
Jas. L. Spangler,	"
Chas. C. Spangler,	"
Samuel W. Hartley,	"
Howard C. Hartley,	"
Willie L. Hildebrand,	"
Augustus Wise,	Abbottstown, Pa.
Jos. W. Shutt,	New Oxford, Pa.

GRADE D.

Lauretta Baker,	East Berlin, Pa.
Alice M. Smith,	"
Bertha Wolf,	"
Mary J. Bender,	"
Lizzie Resser,	"
Michael Hoover,	"
Curtis Spangler,	"
Chas. S. Wolfe,	"
Samuel W. Shaffer,	"
Chas. Baum,	"
Luther Picking,	Thomasville, Pa.

OPENING OF SCHOOL.

This occurred on the 29th of March, 1875, and the catalogue exhibits the attendance during the term.

Large additions will be made for next session. The building will be furnished with new furniture, apparatus, &c.

This institution is located in the midst of a beautiful section of country, remarkable for its healthfulness, and for the picturesque scenery surrounding it.

We have a daily mail, a Literary Society, a large number of papers and journals.

The branches of study are, for next session:

A AND B GRADE.—Reading, Orthography, Penmanship, Written and Mental Arithmetic, Algebra, Geometry, Drawing, History, Political and Physical Geography, Vocal Music, Theory of Teaching, Physiology, Philosophy, and Grammar.

C GRADE.—Reading, Orthography, Penmanship, Written and Mental Arithmetic, Drawing, History, Geography, Grammar, and Vocal Music.

Special rates for German, Latin, Greek, and Instrumental Music.

East Berlin Select School.

J. CURTIS HILDEBRAND,
PRINCIPAL.

The 12th session of this Institution will commence on Monday, the 27th day of March, 1876, and continue 18 weeks with a vacation of five weeks during the months of June and July. Thorough instruction will be given in all the branches generally taught in the higher schools. Special opportunities afforded to those preparing to teach. Pupils can have access to the School Library of over 600 volumes.

As the number is limited early application must be made. Board can be had at reasonable rates. For terms, &c., address the Principal, at East Berlin, Pa.

RECOMMENDATIONS.

I take pleasure in saying that I consider J. Curtis Hildebrand an earnest, faithful and devoted teacher, and his school one of the very best in the county.

AARON SHEELY,
County Superintendent.
Gettysburg, Pa., Oct. 8th 1875.

J. Curtis Hildebrand taught the East Berlin High school during the 2½ years that I was School Superintendent of Adams county. I visited his school a number of times. Mr. Hildebrand was a live, energetic competent, successful and thorough teacher. His school was a model in every respect. In one of my official reports to the Department at Harrisburg, I gave Mr. H the credit of having the best of the 161 schools in the county. This fact expresses briefly, yet fully the estimate which I held of Mr. H. and his school.

J. HOWARD WERT,
Ex-County Superintendent.
Gettysburg, Dec. 3d, 1878.

It is with pleasure that I recommend J. Curtis Hildebrand as a teacher, having known him as such for the past six years. Besides being a well qualified teacher, he is a gentlemen of most excellent character, and I feel confident that any trust confided to him will be faithfully executed.

P. D. W. HANKEY,
Ex-County Superintendent of Adams county.

For a number of years I have known J. Curtis Hildebrand, and have always found him an earnest and zealous worker in the cause of education during this period. I have known many who, through his teachings, have made such rapid improvement that my faith and confidence in him as an educator have become established. I can, therefore, heartily recommend him and his teaching to all parents and guardians who may have children or wards to educate.

R. N. MEISENHELDER, M. D.
East Berlin, Pa.

It affords me pleasure to testify to the excellent moral character of J. Curtis Hildebrand, of East Berlin, Pa., whose intellectual acquirements and experience eminently qualify him for the position of instructor of youth, and I cheerfully recommend him to the confidence of parents and guardians who have children or wards to educate.

DANIEL J. HAUER, D. D.
Hanover, Pa., Dec. 9th, 1878.

This certifies that J. Curtis Hildebrand is a gentleman of high moral character, and in every respect fitted to instruct the youth.

F. C. WOLF, M. D.
East Berlin, Pa.

This certifies that the East Berlin Select school is pleasantly situated and in every way calculated to please and attract. The Principal, J. Curtis Hildebrand, is an experienced and successful teacher, as well as a thorough scholar. Few men, in my judgment, are gifted with the practical tact of communicating knowledge to the student as he is. I feel confident that if parents will give the school a trial by sending their sons and daughters, they will be amply rewarded in the progress of their education.

REV. W. F. P. DAVIS.
Reading, Pa.

I take pleasure in stating that I have been present at the recitations of the school taught in East Berlin, Pa., by Mr. J. Curtis Hildebrand. I was greatly delighted at the drill and discipline of the school. The recitations and training of the classes evinced the fact that Mr. Hildebrand is in a very high degree "apt to teach." The drill in outline map exercises and in general history I never saw equalled. Such results in a school argue great care, skill and patience in the teaching, and these qualities Mr. H's success shows him to be endowed with.

REV. JESSE B. YOUNG,
Pastor of M. E. Church, Gettysburg, Pa.
Dec. 6th, 1878.

I cheerfully recommend Mr. J. Curtis Hildebrand, of East Berlin, Pa., as an efficient and well qualified school-teacher, and of good moral and christian character. Besides the common school term, he has also a number of years been creditably engaged as principal of a select school to prepare young men and ladies for teaching.

AARON SPANGLER,
Minister of the Reformed church.
Jan. 30th, 1875.

Compiler Book and Job Office, Gettysburg, Pa.

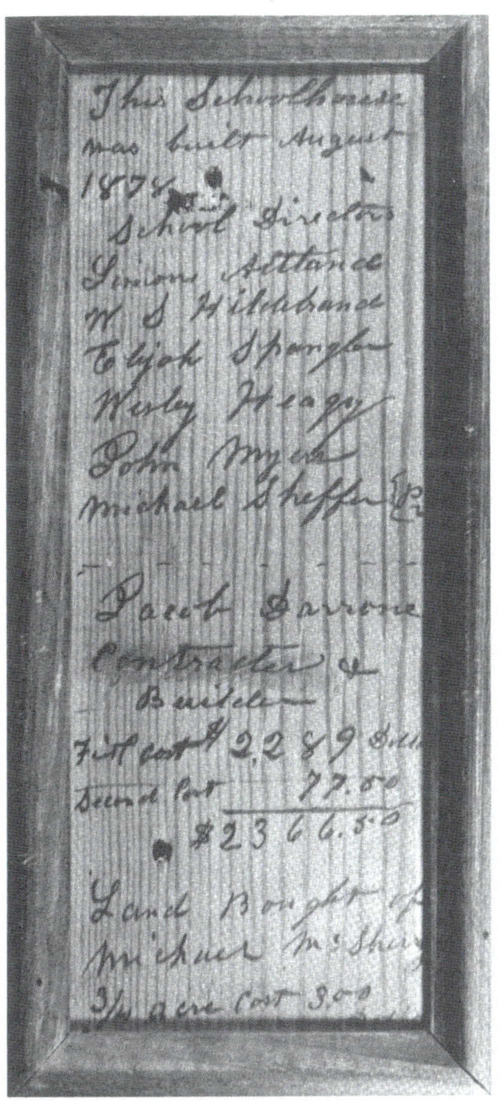

As the population of the town increased, additional school facilities became necessary. Consequently, in 1878 a two-story brick building — 60 by 31 feet — was erected on a three-quarter acre plot purchased from Michael McSherry for three dollars.

This building was erected on the site of the elementary school currently in use; the northeast portion of that building still remains.

The building was first occupied Monday, October 29, 1878 by the East Berlin High and Primary Schools. *High School*, as it is referred to here, was really a grammar school. J. Curtis Hildebrand was principal; Miss Ida M. Hartley was the teacher of the Primary Department. The total enrollment was 122 pupils.

The East Berlin Normal School was founded in 1879, and classes were held in this same building for sixteen weeks during the summer. The faculty in charge of the school was composed of: J. C. Hildebrand, Dr. F. C. Wolf, William J. Metzler, Charles S. Deardorff, and Miss Annie Storm. John H. Nitchman and Kate L. Miller were assistant teachers.

In 1907, the first East Berlin High School recognized by the State was organized. This was a two-year high school with John Harlacher as principal and teacher. In 1909, the first class was graduated and consisted of the following three members: Pauline Tschop, Bessie Walters, and Kathryn Zinn. No classes were graduated in 1910 and 1913 due to lack of pupils those years.

HIGH SCHOOL ENROLLMENT OF 1908

FRONT ROW: A. W. Resser, J. Harlacher, R. W. Trimmer, D. B. Mummert, C. B. Mummert, M. Hildebrand, C. Sweeney, R. Tschop *BACK ROW:* B. Kershner, L. Darone, K. Zinn, P. Tschop, B. Eisenhart, M. Myers, P. Trimmer, A. March *Absent:* B. Walters *Principal:* John E. Harlacher.

In 1923, East Berlin High School became a three-year institution with E. M. Gruver serving as the chief school administrator. Miss Kathryn Wilson (Wentz) was added as a teacher this same year making a faculty of two. Again, no class was graduated because of the extra year being added. An additional room was needed for high school classes; so, the little school by the cemetery which had been closed in 1916 was reopened to house the primary grades. This building was permanently closed for school purposes in 1930, at which time the main school building was renovated and four new classrooms were added since the primary grades returned. One of the original rooms was converted to indoor toilets.

In 1933, East Berlin High School became a first-class or four-year high school, with J. Harold Little serving as principal. As a result, no class was graduated that year.

Additional facilities were needed; consequently, in 1936 three classrooms, a gymnatorium, and an office were added to the existing building.

As the enrollment increased and the curriculum was expanded, additional classrooms became a necessity. To remedy this situation, a three-room concrete block building was erected to the west of the main structure in 1945, to house the elementary grades.

In 1947, the Junior-Senior High School was organized, including grades seven through twelve. In the same year, a three-room temporary building was constructed.

On July 1, 1948, the Conewago Joint School System was formed by Abbottstown Borough, East Berlin Borough, Conewago Independent School District, and Reading Township, of Adams County, and Paradise Township of York County. At this time, four one-room schools were in operation in Paradise Township, three in Reading Township, a three-room building in Abbottstown, and four rooms in East Berlin. These rooms and buildings housed grades one through six, with seventh and eighth grades attending the Junior-Senior High School in East Berlin. Conewago Independent School had been closed in 1938 with all pupils attending school in East Berlin.

Time passed; all elementary pupils and many high school students continued to be housed in substandard and inadequate buildings, while the member boards bickered over a building program. Finally, by court order, the Jointure was dissolved as of July 1, 1957.

Later that same year, Conewago Independent School District, East Berlin Borough, and Reading Township became a part of the Bermudian Springs Joint School System which included Huntington Township, Latimore Township, and York Springs Borough. (Conewago Independent District has since been dissolved and is now a part of Reading Township for school purposes. 1962)

The Bermudian Springs School Authority was formed almost simultaneously with the formation of the Jointure by the three original member districts. Its purpose was to provide the necessary facilities for the students of the Joint School System. The first building program was the remodeling and expansion of the York Springs School where six classrooms, an all-purpose room, cafeteria kitchen, and office were added. This project was completed in 1958 at a cost of $380,000.

The second building program was the remodeling and addition to the East Berlin School. This project was approved by the Department of Public Instruction on July 22, 1958. Authority was given to construct five classrooms and a kitchen, also to renovate eight classrooms, office area and a multi-purpose room. This project was completed in August, 1960 at a cost of $237,896.48. With the completion of this project, all one-room schools had been closed at the end of the 1959-60 school year.

Approval for the construction of Bermudian Springs Junior-Senior High School, to be located on Route 94 approximately two miles south of York Springs, was also granted in 1958. Construction was begun in October, 1959; and the building was ready for occupancy on February 15, 1961. On that date, the high school students from the East Berlin and York Springs Units were moved into the new school, the first school in the State to be electrically heated. Within a matter of days, all elementary students were moved from the remaining substandard buildings into the new and renovated facilities in East Berlin and York Springs.

Except for the concrete block building, which is used for storage and the Scouts Program, all temporary and substandard buildings have been disposed of. Certainly, great strides have been made in a comparatively short period of time.

ELEMENTARY SCHOOL — 1964

Getting an Early Start

Recess

Back to work in the Opportunity Room.

Library Time

End of the Day

Agriculture Shop

BERMUDIAN SPRINGS HIGH SCHOOL 1964

The Teacher

Cafeteria

Library

Hall

EDUCATIONAL PROGRESS

1769 — First English School opened
1769 — *1838:* Church-operated schools
1836 — Berlin Improvement Society founded
1839 — First public school
1870 — Select Academy established
1878 — Two-story brick building erected
1879 — East Berlin Normal School founded
1907 — First East Berlin high school recognized by the State
1909 — First class graduated from East Berlin High School
1910 — No graduating class due to lack of pupils
1913 — No graduating class due to lack of pupils
1923 — Three-year high school; no graduating class; baseball became a varsity sport
1930 — Building renovated — four rooms added, indoor toilets installed; church school house permanently closed
1933 — Four-year high school; no graduating class; soccer introduced
1935 — Orchestra formed
1936 — Construction of gymnatorium and office; three classrooms added; commercial course added; alumni association formed; basketball introduced
1937 — School band organized; course in agriculture offered
1938 — First art teacher employed
1941 — Home Economics added to the curriculum
1942 — Girls' basketball championship (league)
1944 — Student council organized
1945 — Concrete-block building constructed
1946 — First school nurse employed
1947 — Junior-Senior High School established; three-room temporary building erected; first high school librarian employed; industrial arts added to curriculum; State champion contralto
1948 — Parent-teacher association formed; Pennsylvania cherry-pie champion; football introduced; Conewago Joint School System formed
1951 — First high school principal; boys' basketball championship (league)
1952 — Boys' basketball District 3 championship
1954 — Driver education introduced
1957 — Conewago Joint School System dissolved; East Berlin became part of Bermudian Springs Joint School System
1958 — First elementary principal; remodeling and expansion of the York Springs School; first guidance counselor employed
1960 — Remodeling and addition to the East Berlin School
1961 — Completion of the Bermudian Springs High School building; first centralized elementary library
1962 — Bermudian Springs High School Alumni Association formed

CHIEF SCHOOL ADMINISTRATORS

1907-1910: John Harlacher
1910-1915: J. W. Bucher
1915-1916: Grund F. Beckmyer
1916-1917: E. M. Gruver
1917-1918: Warren H. Cocklin
David M. Crist
1918-1919: Daniel Ruff
1919-1920: Harper Wentz
1920-1922: Raymond H. Fissel
1922-1926: E. M. Gruver
1926-1934: J. Harold Little
1934-1956: E. M. Gruver
1956-1957: Thomas A. Schade
1957- : Amos D. Meyers

HIGH SCHOOL PRINCIPALS

1951-1954: Charles W. Hash *1954-1956:* Thomas A. Schade *1957- :* Alfred R. Billett

ELEMENTARY PRINCIPAL

1958- : Charles R. Philips

BERMUDIAN SPRINGS SCHOOL DISTRICT

The Bermudian Springs School District occupies 75 square miles of Adams County's rolling hills of beautiful orchards and farmlands between Gettysburg and Dillsburg. This rural setting includes the boroughs of East Berlin and York Springs, as well as the townships of Huntington, Latimore, Reading and part of Hamilton. The 1990 Department of Commerce census totals over 11,500 inhabitants.

Adams County is known as the "Apple Capital" of the United States and is the home of the brand names, "Lucky Leaf', "Mott's" and "Musselman's." Many area businesses are related to the fruit industry, including box manufacturers, packing houses, nurseries, trucking firms, orchard material suppliers and equipment dealers. The Pennsylvania State University Fruit Research Laboratory is located in nearby Biglerville.

Significant points of interest in the area are the Gettysburg National Military Park and the Eisenhower National Historic Site. The nearby Appalachian Trail, Pennsylvania State Park lands, Ski Liberty Resort, Ski Roundtop, and several golf courses offer a wide range of recreational opportunities. The Bermudian Springs School District is located within easy access to the Metropolitan and culture centers of Baltimore, MD; Harrisburg/Hershey, PA; and Washington, D.C. Nearby institutions of higher learning include: Gettysburg College, the Lutheran Theological Seminary at Gettysburg, Dickinson College, the Army War College, the Mount Alto Campus of Penn State University, Harrisburg Campus of Penn State University, Harrisburg Area Community College and Western Maryland College.

CAMPUS FACILITY IMPROVEMENTS

An "educational campus" was created...

Before 1978, the high school housed grades 7 thru 12, and the ele-mentary schools in York Springs and East Berlin housed grades K thru 6. In 1978, a new middle school was constructed to house grades 5 thru 8. This changed the high school configuration to grades 9 thru 12, and the old elementary schools remained grades K thru 4.

In 1990-1991, the new elementary school was constructed. In that year, both elementary schools in York Springs and East Berlin were closed.

In 1993-1994, the middle school was added on to: classrooms and an auxiliary gym. The original high school façade was covered over with a tan stucco-look to better insulate the building. The library was moved to inside the courtyard. The "300 wing" was constructed, adding 8 additional classrooms and maintenance storage underneath.

In 2006-2008, major renovations to the high school were made. The 1993-1994 tan school façade was stripped off and re-walled and re-windowed with a new gray exterior. Hallways and classrooms were re-configured. Electrical wiring and plumbing were brought up to code. The original gymnasium wing was torn down. Two gymnasiums and related locker and storage rooms were built in the new sports wing.
A wrestling practice area was now part of the high school facility. The large parking lot once located behind the high school (between the old cafeteria and shop building) was eliminated. A whole new classroom wing was built in its place to house a new cafeteria, home-economics, art room, industrial arts rooms, vo-ag rooms, etc. The entire building was now air-conditioned.

The high school administration offices were shifted to the front of the building. The original auditorium was gutted, and new cushioned seats, AC, lighting, storage room etc. were installed along with a new Large Group Instruction room next door where a small outdoor courtyard once stood.

In 2014, a new water pre-treatment system was installed for all three buildings.

ATHLETIC TIMELINE

During the Summer of 1990, brand new home bleachers, press box, and concession stand/ restrooms were added to the football field complex.

During the Summer of 1993, a brand new football scoreboard was installed.

During the Summer of 1995, stadium lights [donated by the Sports Boosters & community] were installed.

During the Summer of 2002, the stadium field was re-leveled and an all-weather track was added at the football stadium.

During the Winter/Spring of 2014-2015, an artificial surface is scheduled to be installed at the football stadium, as well as a new artificial surface on a brand-new soccer/field hockey/softball field.

During the Summer of 1978, the two tennis courts that used to be located between the high school parking lot and the sewer plant were replaced by the four tennis courts now located near the high school football scoreboard.

During the Summer of 2005, a brand-new baseball scoreboard was installed...paid for by the Sports Boosters, the baseball team, and business donations.

At the conclusion of the 2006-2007 winter sports season, the 46-year-old high school gymnasium was destined for demolition. To finish out the school year, all high school gymnasium-related activities were shifted to the Middle School. Demolition of the old H.S. gymnasium started around February 15, 2007, to make way for the new 2-gymnasium facility.

All 2007-2008 winter sports were played in the elementary schoolor middle school gymnasiums.

The 2008-2009 Volleyball Team was the first BSHS sport to compete in the NEW gymnasium.

During the Summer of 2011...The 33-year-old tennis courts were rebuilt. A new "blue and green" surface, nets, and exterior fencing were installed.

During the Summer of 2014...The School Board approved pre-liminary construction plans for the two new artificial playing fields planned for the fall of 2015 usage.

BERMUDIAN SPRINGS
HIGH SCHOOL
EAGLES ATHLETICS

BERMUDIAN SPRINGS
HOME
INNING
GUESTS
BALL
STRIKE
OUT
H E

INTERSCHOLASTIC SPORTS

since 1965...

Between 1965 and 1998, the following sports were available for Bermudian Springs students to participate in:

Fall: **field hockey, football, volleyba ll, cross-country, cheerleading**

Winter: **boys basketball, girls basketball, wrestling, cheerleading**

Spring: **boys track, girls track, boys baseball, girls softball**

In the 1998-1999 school year, boys soccer and golf were added.

In the 2011-2012 school year, girls tennis was added.

In the 2012-2013 school year, girls soccer was added.

There has been only one STATE Championship Team for Bermudian Springs: The baseball game was played at Blair County Ballpark, Altoona, PA at 10:30 AM on Friday, June 18, 2010

Bermudian Springs "Eagles"
beat Martinsburg Central "Scarlet Dragons" [a.k.a. Spring Cove School District] with a score of 5 to 3 to become Class AA – 2010 State Baseball Champions

CHAMPIONSHIP TEAMS SINCE 2000

Boys Soccer...League Champs...04-05
Girls Soccer...League Champs...07-08,09-10

Field Hockey...
League Champs... 04-05,05-06,07-08,08-09,09-10,13-14

Football...
League Champs...06-07,08-09,11-12,12-13
District Champs...92-93,93-94,98-99

Boys Cross Country...League Champs...08-09

Wrestling...
League Champs... 01-02,02-03,,03-04,05-06,06-07,07-08,09-10,10-11,22-12,12-13,13-14
District Champs...03-04,04-05,07-08,10-11
"Team" Champs...99-00, 03-04,07-08

Boys Basketball...League Champs...13-14
Girls Basketball...League Champs...03-04

Baseball...
League Champs...07-08,08-09,09-10
District Champs...09-10
STATE Champs...09-10

Boys Track...League Champs...08-09
Softball...League Champs...09-10

BUSINESS

BUSINESS

Up from the depths of the earth and its unknown source comes that ever-precious water to form a cool and refreshing spring. As the soft melodious trickle flows over its gentle banks and begins to form a brook, it winds its way down the hillside and through the valleys to join its companions. Melting snow and drizzling rain seep through the woodland and open fields to add to the size of the stream. As it progresses and grows, it gathers strength and develops into bubbling rapids devoid of bland earth. Under a man-made structure it flows, relinquishing its power for the use of God's children in their incessant struggle to progress. On it flows; spent of its strength, it is contented to retire in a deep placid pool to view other surrounding wonders of nature.

MILLS

EAST BERLIN MILL

Peter Lehn, a German, erected his mill on the Conewago Creek at the West end of Berlin in 1769.

Michael Geiselman who owned and operated the mill from 1823 to 1846 was listed as a grist, saw and plasterer miller. His heir operated it until 1848.

Others who owned and operated this mill were: Samuel S. Sprenkle, Jacob N. Hershey, Elam Siegrist, Aaron Siegrist, Issac Siegrist, S. Morgan Smith and Charles Rebert. Michael Rebert owned and operated the mill from 1887 to 1905. When Michael Rebert took ownership of the mill in 1887, he built the first large dam on the Conewago Creek and dug the mill race leading into the mill.

During the great flood of 1889, (better known as the Johnstown Flood) the mill, as well as the farm on which the Reberts lived, was damaged. The greatest damage to the mill came twelve years later when a fire destroyed practically all of the mill. After this fire of 1901, the mill was rebuilt and sold in 1905 to Noah Sell. Mr. Sell owned and operated the mill until 1925 when he sold it to Elmer B. Eisenhart and John R. Gentzler. On August 24, 1933 water reached a depth of eighteen inches on the grinding floor and caused immense damage to the stock from flooding. Eisenhart and Gentzler sold the mill to T. C. and R. F. Owings in 1938.

On March 1, 1960 fire completely destroyed a large part of the building. Many changes and expansions have occurred since then. Richard O. Riggs, president of the milling company, now employs 32 people and produces 500 tons of finished feed each week. The present mill stands on the same sight as the Peter Lehn Mill of 1769.

EISENHART'S MILL

The tract of land on which the Eisenhart Mill is located was first deeded to Peter Ouler in 1747 by Thomas and Richard Penn; it was known as *Ouler's Richland.* After several transfers, the tract was acquired by Christian Class in 1762. A stone house on the farm is still used as a dwelling place and bears the inscription *C. C. 1766.*

The real estate of Conrad Eisenhart II included several tracts of land in West Manchester, Washington and North Codorus Townships of York County.

The Washington Township tract included a grist mill, which was acquired from the estate of Jacob Welsh in 1824. He sold same to Emanuel Butt in 1848. Conrad's will stipulated that his son, Peter, should buy the Washington Township property at $4000.

A great-grandson, Elmer, purchased this property from his father, Frank, in 1922 and owns it at the present time. Elmer has been a miller all his life, starting at the age of 15. He worked in his father's mill; and now at the age of 87, he is found at his place of business each day.

HAMILTON ROLLER MILLS

Hamilton Roller Mills, located in Hamilton Township, was owned by W. W. Hafer; this site included a saw mill and flour and feed machinery.

Those who operated the mill were: Elmer Eisenhart, 1903; Albert Stambaugh, 1904-1907 — during this period, Rolandus Kunkle who lived on the nearby farm, was killed on the saw mill; Charles Butt, 1907-1910; Robert Hartman, 1910-1917; John E. Gentzler, 1917-1922. The business was discontinued after 1922.

Elmer Eisenhart purchased the mill, which he dismantled about 1928; he erected another building early in 1932.

JACOBS' MILL

The first mill was built by George Jacobs about 1772 on Beaver Creek in Paradise Township, York County. The original homestead farm property and the mill property have never been owned by anyone other than members of the Jacobs' family.

Amos G. Jacobs purchased the very first turbine ever built by S. Morgan Smith of nearby York in August of 1877.

In this mill they ground feed, made flour, sawed logs and made flannel for women's dresses and cassinettes (waistcoating) for men's clothes. The mill was equipped with carding and spinning machines, looms, and full stocks for shrinking.

The mill was last run about 1932 by Birdes Jacobs for *chopping* feed and sawing logs; it was torn down about December 1942. The building that was razed in 1942 was the third mill that was erected on this site.

The farm property is now owned by William C. Jacobs of York; the mill property is owned by Mrs. Nettie E. Baughman of Dover.

SWEIGART'S MILL

This stone building was erected in 1794 by Abraham Sweigart; the building is still intact. John Nagle, the mason who constructed the mill, left his name and the date of erection on a large stone tablet in the west end of the mill.

Abraham and Eleanor Sweigart, of Hamilton and Paradise Townships, sold the Beaver Creek Mill to Ludwig Schwartz and his son, John, 1811 for the sum of $5000. The mill was equipped to process flour and feed.

In 1831, Ludwig and John Schwartz sold the mill — 96 acres, 114 perches — for $9500 to John Smith of Mount Pleasant Township in Adams County.

The mill and farm were purchased later by George Jacobs and is presently owned by his grandson, Carlton Jacobs. The mill is no longer in operation.

FACTORIES

BRUSH FACTORY

A small, three-story building was used as a brush factory operated by the Hartman family, who retired sometime before 1909. One of the daughters was married to Doctor Hoechst of East Berlin. The factory stood where Adam Myers' house now stands.

CANNERIES

A canning factory which processed corn was located on Locust Street. The factory was owned and operated by Benjamin Mehring and Brother; canning was done here sometime between 1920 and 1929.

****

Another canning factory which processed tomatoes was also located on Locust Street and operated between 1935 and 1939.

CARRIAGE, WAGON, AUTOMOBILE INDUSTRIES

The Benjamin Krall home on West King Street, formerly the Nevin Brown home, was a carriage-building factory early in 1800. After work discontinued, the building was converted into a double house which the Kralls purchased in 1953.

****

Adam Miller built and sold carriages on Harrisburg Street.

****

Studebaker Blacksmith Forge

North of Hunterstown, Pennsylvania, stood the old Studebaker Blacksmith Forge used by John, father of the famous Studebaker Brothers who were manufacturers of wagons and automobiles.

This was America's first vehicle manufacturer, starting business in 1852 and continuing until recent months.

Two of the five brothers who founded the company were born close to East Berlin. Clement was the name of the one son.

In 1853, the first Studebaker transport vehicle completed the hazardous cross-continent trip to California.

The Blacksmith Shop was torn down in 1959.

GARMENT FACTORIES

Ursinus Glatfelter had a sewing factory on Locust Street from 1899 to 1928.

****

The East Berlin Garment Company, owned and operated by Julius Bernstein, opened December 3, 1951 with eighteen female employees; at present, approximately fifty ladies are employed by this firm. The factory operations began with the manufacture of blouses; but in 1960, the production changed to girls' dresses.

SHOE FACTORIES

The Hake Shoe Company was operated in 1925 in a building owned by Cletus Mummert located on West King Street.

****

After the Hake Shoe Company terminated production, the Brown Shoe Factory, operated by Clark Brown, functioned from 1930 to 1933.

****

The East Berlin Shoe Company is a branch of the Gettysburg Shoe Company. In 1959, plans were made for further expansion; and the East Berlin site was selected. Operations began in early 1960, and the employment figure has now reached approximately three hundred fifty.

The factory produces mostly children's and misses' shoes; but, in addition, this branch factory supplies essential parts of all types of shoes to all of the company's factories.

TANNERY

Vat for soaking hides.

John Hildebrand, Sr., who lived across the Conewago Creek, was proprietor of the Tannery for many years. Hildebrand's daughter, Sarah, married Henry Picking who erected a store in the house of William S. Hildebrand. Later, a new building was built on the property of Mrs. P. B. Kauffman, where he continued in business until 1823. They moved to Westmoreland County in 1826.

WOOD PRODUCTS

In October of 1943, one Newell E. Coxon purchased an old frame building from Cletus Mummert. Without financial aid from the town or townspeople, he set out to renovate the building and begin manufacturing operations.

The first operations of Penn Wood were limited to covering heels which were sent in from other plants, while machinery was being installed. However, by the end of the same year, work was underway in all departments.

As production grew, the supply of raw material became inadequate. The shortage of dry lumber during these war years led to the building of the first two dry kilns. In 1947, residents were on hand to see another *first* for East Berlin; a charge of thoroughly processed and dried lumber emerging from the kiln.

The successful operation of the kilns led to the construction of two more units in 1955. The volume of dry lumber being processed necessitated the construction of a large warehouse for its storage.

FARMING

He gave man birth from the dust of the earth;
Man lives by it; and then returns.
He kissed the earth with His blessings,
And delivered unto man the substance of life.
He pours from the heavens the moisture and energy to produce growth;
He gave the plants the right to propagate and multiply.
He developed the cycle of food and life,
And placed man in the hub for preservations.
He gave man the necessities,
And asked only for his children to live in abundance.
He delivered unto man the intelligence to use His earth for the promotion of man-kind.
The gifts of God have been plentiful!

****

But have we given Him the derserving thanks for the bounties of life we enjoy? This, each one of us must answer in our own way.

The next few pages is our way of saying thanks to our fellowman for his part in caring for the bounties of life which we enjoy.

It became apparent that more innovations in the handling of lumber were necessary to stay competitive. This led to the installation of a machine which was affectionately named, *Newell's Folly.* More correctly, it is known as a Moore-Tilting Load Unstacker and Chain Arm Stacker. This installation was the first of its kind in Pennsylvania.

Following the untimely death of Newell Coxon on September 15, 1958, the business was carried on through the efforts of Mrs. Newell Coxon and Mrs. Hazel Hoffman. After the completion of college and the fulfillment of miltary obligations, the eldest son of the founder, Newell, Jr., assumed a full-time role in the management of the business.

In January 1962, negotiations were completed for the sale of the heel manufacturing division. At this time, the lumber division assumed the name of Penn Wood Products Company. In August of 1962, Penn Wood Products moved into its new office quarters.

In 1963, the Penn Wood Products Company purchased the additional three acres of land to increase its storage capacity of green lumber.

****

Beau Products, Incorporated, is a subsidiary of Penn Wood Products Company.

When Penn Wood found that some items of lumber were difficult to move in the rough, Mr. Newell Coxon, Sr., checked the possibilities of markets for semi-finished wood parts and mouldings. He determined that there were markets for such items. It was further determined that these items could in part be manufactured out of some species and grades of lumber which otherwise were not in demand.

In 1952, the first moulding machine was put into operation. Like any new venture, the first years were difficult ones. As time passed and proficiency and skill were acquired, the products were more refined; and a more competitive position was assumed.

By 1960, four moulding machines were in operation.

In 1962, an addition was made to the existing building which provided more working and storage space as well as the space to install a Double Surface Planing Machine.

****

William Leas had a saw mill and lumber yard on Locust Street in 1880; he built and operated the spoke factory shown here.

HARVEST TIME

MAKING HAY

A Hurricane Destroys a Barn and Hay Crop.

Did anyone find a *red* ear?

Rollin' over the corn stubbles.

The *'tater* patch.

Spreadin' it for Spring.

Bossy and friends coming home to fill the pails.

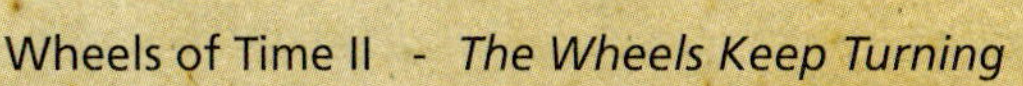

Photos provided with permission of Kelly Mummert Hollabaugh

MUMMERT FARMS

In 2005 the Mummert Farm located on Peepytown Road was designated a Bicentennial Farm by the Pennsylvania Department of Agriculture. It has been in the Mummert family for over 200 years. The farm is referred to as the "Peninsula", as it is surrounded by the Conewago Creek on three sides and it is basically the same as when it was deeded in 1789. As of 2014, there are five of Wayne and Shirley Mummert's grandchildren living on the farm, representing the ninth generation.

THE SEBRIGHT FARM

located at 1614 Germany Road in East Berlin, Adams County, was originally purchased in two separate tracts by Lewis Detter on March 22, 1866, and March 27, 1872. The farm has since progressed from Lewis Detter to his son-in-law, William Sebright, to William's son Raymond Sebright, to Raymond's son Rodney Sebright, and now to Rodney's son Robby Sebright. Robby currently resides on the original farmstead, with his wife Jayne and three sons, George, Charles and Edward. Robby and Jane's three sons represent the sixth generation on the farm. The farm currently operates as a dairy and crop farm.

PUBLIC SALE

DEMONSTRATION - FORDSON TRACTOR - {ABBOTTSTOWN - 1921 -
- FARMER'S PICNIC - {AND EAST BERLIN}

SERVICE

EAST BERLIN NATIONAL BANK

In the early part of the month of May in 1903, a group of local citizens met in the East Berlin Fire Engine House for the purpose of organizing a new bank for East Berlin. Eighteen of these men subscribed to $25,000 Capital Stock for the bank. The following May 15th the shareholders met and elected the first Board of Directors consisting of seven shareholders, as follows: John Bosserman, W. G. Leas, G. Emanuel Spotz, P. C. Smith, I. H. Hoechst, A. B. Mummert and C. C. Spangler. The new Board of Directors organized by naming the following officers: President, P. C. Smith; Vice President, I. H. Hoechst; Cashier, I. S. Miller. Charles S. Duncan was selected as attorney for the bank. At a later date, L. K. Baker was named as Teller.

The original Certificate of Organization is dated, May 27, 1903, indicating that all of the requirements of the Office of the Comptroller of the Currency had been completed and the new organization was entitled to a Charter. The minutes of July 30, 1903 indicate that the Charter was granted and The East Berlin National Bank was authorized to open for business on August 10, 1903. On the day of the opening of the new bank, the assets of the W. G. Leas private bank were merged with The East Berlin National Bank; and the new bank conducted its business in the building on the south side of West King Street; the building was owned by W. G. Leas.

In March of 1907, a building committee was appointed to look into the matter of erecting a new bank building since the original quarters had become inadequate for the business of the bank. On May 27, 1907 this committee, consisting of I. S. Miller, P. C. Smith and I. H. Hoechst accepted the bid of A. B. Trimmer to build the new building on the northwest corner of West King and Fourth Streets. The banking business and equipment were moved to the new building on February 12, 1908.

During the year 1926, the building was remodeled. New furniture and fixtures, new heating facilities and a new vault were installed. The bank is doing business in the same building at present.

In the early days of March 1933, banks throughout the Nation ceased operations by Presidential Proclamation, due to the existing financial crisis. During the period following the *Nationwide Bank Holiday,* this bank operated on a restricted basis and proceeded to reorganize. New Capital Stock of $50,000 was subscribed to by 309 local citizens. These shareholders elected the following ten men to serve as the first Board of Directors: O. S. Hoffman, M. B. Burgard, Joseph E. Renoll, Charles S. Myers, R. O. Nell, John H. Gise, I. J. Mummert, Adam C. Myers, Curvin P. Shaffer, George M. Hummer. On March 22, 1934, the Board of Directors met and organized as follows: President, O. S. Hoffman; Vice President, M. B. Burgard; Secretary, Joseph E. Renoll; Cashiers, C. D. Krout and Assistant, N. A. Decker. A new charter, under the name East Berlin National Bank, was granted by the Comptroller of the Currency on April 4, 1934. The bank opened for business on April 9, 1934 with resources of $329,000 which have since grown to nearly $3,000,000.

C. D. Krout served continuously as Cashier from the opening date in 1934 until January, 1962 at which time he was elected President succeeding the late M. B. Burgard. At this same time, Charles L. Spangler was elected as Cashier. Present Board of Directors consists of: C. D. Krout, M. D. Jacobs, R. J. Jacobs, Jesse Gentzler, Charles L. Spangler and Irvin B. Mummert. Present officers are: President, C. D. Krout; Vice President, M. D. Jacobs; Secretary, R. J. Jacobs; Cashier, Charles L. Spangler. Helen Altland and Ruth Cook are serving as tellers and bookkeepers.

PEOPLES STATE BANK

About 1911, a number of people in town and the surrounding community decided that there was a need for another bank. On March 17, 1911 The People's State Bank was opened for business in the house on the corner of East King and Harrisburg Streets, which was used for many years as a hardware store operated by D. A. March. The interior of the building has been altered several times to meet the needs of the expanding business.

The new bank had a capital of twenty-five thousand dollars. On June 27, 1946 the capital was increased to fifty thousand dollars. Noah Sell was the first bank president, followed by Freizer Altland, Dr. T. C. Miller, P. Lawrence Hoover and the present president, S. E. Altland. William P. Baker was the first cashier with D. A. March acting as his assistant. Mr. Baker retired after serving for twenty-nine years. His successors were: Paul Schwartz, Robert W. Myers, Q. R. Ellis, Charles H. Lawver, J. Bruce McClay and John R. Wisler.

At the present time, John R. Wisler is Cashier; Keith H. Gladfelter, Assistant Cashier; Harriet C. Myers, Dorothy M. Roomsburg and Joyce E. Eisenhart, Tellers. S. A. Altland is President; J. Monroe Danner, J. Monroe Anthony, Jonas Gruver, George R. Gladfelter, Carlton L. Jacobs and Harry R. Mummert are the other members of the Board of Directors.

Apparently, the people of the community have looked favorably on the policies and management of the bank. It has a steady and uninterrupted growth of over fifty-two years. It is now over a three-million-dollar corporation.

2014

SUSQUEHANNA BANK

At Susquehanna Bank, building enduring relationships with customers is the key to success. For more than a century, businesses and families have been relying on Susquehanna Bank to help them save, borrow and invest. Over the years, the bank's team has developed valuable experience that they put to work for customers each day.

Founded in 1901, the bank has grown to encompass more than 260 branches in Maryland, Pennsylvania, New Jersey, and West Virginia. In the town of East Berlin, our roots go back to 1911 when People's State Bank was opened for business on the corner of East King and Harrisburg Streets, which was used for many years as a hardware store operated by D. A. March. The interior of the building has been altered several times to meet the needs of the expanding business. Susquehanna Bank is part of Susquehanna Bancshares, Inc., a holding company that also includes subsidiaries that offer other valuable financial services, such as commercial leasing, asset management, insurance, retirement planning and pension programs for businesses.

Susquehanna Bank offers a wide variety of loans and financing for expansion, construction and operating equipment. The bank is an SBA Preferred Lender. For small business lines of credit, it offers standardized terms, simplified applications and streamlined processing to allow for quick review of loan applications. The bank also offers an array of services for consumers, from deposit accounts and loans to mortgage services. Susquehanna Bank continually works to offer greater convenience, and customers can take advantage of internet, mobile and text banking services.

BARBERS

Claude Lapham

Claude Lapham was one of the early barbers in town. He was well known by the people of the community for his many other talents aside from barbering. Other barbers who have been of service to the community include: Pat McCue, Harry Lory, Maurice Lookinbill, Rolandus Himes, Robert Zeigler, Mr. Dugan, Clarence Gochenauer, and Lester Davis.

One of our barbers Lavere Burgard, better known as "La," has given dependable service to our community for many years. Recently, Earl Zeigler opened a shop on West King Street.

MORTICIANS

Jacob Darone	1890
Andrew Trimmer	1890-1918
Calvin Fohl	1914-1919
Harry Emig	1919-1941

Mr. Bohn, a mortician, lived three doors from the square on the north side of East King Street and had his Parlor in the same building about the turn of the century.

Richard C. (Dick) Emig assumed the operation of his father's business in 1941 and is serving our community at present.

Harry Emig's Funeral Home

2014

ZEIGLER'S BARBER SHOP

Proprietor, Earl E. Zeigler opened his shop in June 1963. The original shop was located at 105 West King Street. The building was owned by Cletus Mummert. In 1977, Zeigler's Barber Shop moved to 120 West King Street. Mr. Zeigler bought the barber shop from previous owner; Lavere Burgard. Zeigler's Barber Shop is still located at 120 W. King Street and owned by Earl Zeigler.

OLD GLORY BARBERSHOP

209 Locust Street East | Berlin, PA 17316

The Old Glory Barbershop and Antique Shop was opened in 1991 by Kim Hagerman and was located on the south side of Center Square in East Berlin. The proprietor focused on hair cutting, hair dyeing and hair styling in general, along with offering selected quality antiques to interested customers. The shop operated in this location for five years.

In 1996, the property at 409 West King Street was purchased by the proprietor and the Old Glory Barber Shop and Antique Shop relocated to a new location. Upon relocation of the business, Martin Menges joined the firm as a second barber and stylist.

During the seven years Old Glory was based at 409 West King Street, a kitchen gift shop, a garden shop and general line of antiques were offered to customers along with a general service line of barber and hair styling services.

During 2003, the Old Glory Barbershop again relocated, this time to 209 Locust Street in East Berlin. The focus of the shop at this third location was entirely on barber-related activities.

Beginning in 2010, Sarah Wolf joined the Old Glory staff as a third barber/stylist.

MICHELANGELO'S HAIR AND NAIL STUDIO

209 Locust Street | East Berlin, PA 17316

717-259-9310

Michelangelo's Hair and Nail Studio originally was owned and operated by Dawn McKean which was located on the North side of the Brandt Warehouse/Mill in East Berlin. Her focus was on hair cutting, hair dyeing, hairstyling and tanning. The shop operated in this location for many years, under Dawn McKean.

When Dawn decided to change professions, the ownership of the business changed; and Heather Neiderer decided she would like to own the beauty salon. Heather Neiderer continues to operate the business at 209 Locust Street at the lower level. Heather Neiderer employs two part-time stylists; Kimberly A. Smith and Kobie Byers. There is also Michelle Hollinger, who is a certified massage therapist.

Michelangelo's continues to offer a variety of hair care products and services, including hair extensions.

Stop in and meet the staff.

Post Office — Dedicated 1960

POST OFFICE

The post office was established in 1827. With the establishment of the post office, it became necessary to change the name of the town from *Berlin* to *East Berlin,* in order to avert any confusion with the town of *Berlin* in the western part of our State.

Christian Picking, became the first Postmaster, and others to follow were:

William Hildebrand	1831	Jacob H. Hildebrand	1893
John Fletcher	1833	Elias L. Kauffman	1897
D. Grumbine	1839	Noah B. Sprenkle	1914
Emanuel Kuhn	1841	John E. Anthony	1922
William Wolf	1845	Noah B. Sprenkle	1930
Robert Hutchinson	1847	Annie Anthony	1930
William Wolf	1853	Merton Himes	1930
J. Wood	1853	Mervin Lau	1935
Francis Hildebrand	1861	Edna Jacobs	1935
Henry S. Hildebrand	1879	Richard Smyers	1952
Abner S. Hildebrand	1886	Lavere Burgard	1953
William Resser	1889	Eugene Elgin	1954

Locations of the Post Offices since 1827:

Jane Urick House — Present occupants, Wilbur Jacobs' family
Dr. Roos' House
Noah Sprenkle's House
Stucco House on south side of West King Street at Third Street
New Post Office building erected in 1960

This Post Office changed from Fourth Class to Presidential appointment July 21, 1920.

RURAL ROUTE CARRIERS

ROUTE #1		ROUTE #2	
Roscoe E. Bosserman	1902	Emerson C. Winand	1902
William Sinner	1920	Francis R. Darone	1922
Lester Brown	1946	Harry E. Serff	1935
Irwin Gross	1956	Leonard L. Myers	1939

EAST BERLIN POST OFFICE RURAL CARRIERS

from 1975 to the present (2014)

Postal cancellation ink stamp offered on May 8th, 2014 by the U.S. Postal Service

Route 1

Mervin Myers
Retired 1977

Lloyd Boyer
Retired 2002

Rodney Hollabaugh,
Current Carrier

Route 2

Leonard Myers
Retired 1981

Wayne Mummert
Retired 1991

Joan Stevens

Susan Kehr,
Current Carrier

Route 3 (created 1983)

Diana Stambaugh
Retired 2005

Joan Stevens,
Current Carrier

Route 4 (created 1994)

Kim Dillon,
Current Carrier

Route 5 (created 1998)

Rodney Hollabaugh

Missy Melhorn,
Current Carrier

Current Substitute Carriers

Nicole May

Ravi Bastola

Clerks

Gladys Singleton

Beth Seitz

Donna Cassatt

Former Clerks

Marilyn Hoover

Sandy Fletcher

Kathy King

Kim Poncavage

Sue Gait

Postmasters

Marilyn Hoover,
Interim Postmaster

Charlie Eisenhart,
Retired 1991

Regina Ballingham,
Interim Postmaster 1991

Anna Renee Yelten
Current Postmaster

C. E. Butt — Mail Wagon and Horse "John," 1906

"Jakie" the unofficial mail carrier in lobby of post office at Third and King Streets.

PROFESSION OF MEDICAL SCIENCE

This house has been the home of several doctor's who have served our community through the years. This has been a doctor's home continuously since the incorporation of the Borough.

MEDICAL DOCTORS

Dr. John B. Arnold	1800-1822
Dr. Thomas Stevens	
Dr. William Wolf	-1877
Dr. Samuel Meisenhelder	1851-1884
Dr. Frederick C. Wolf	1865-1907
Dr. Edmund W. Meisenhelder	1868-1871
Dr. Robeht Meisenhelder	1871-1890
Dr. Daniel L. Baker	1881-
Dr. Lewis Fackler	1886-1901
Dr. Harleigh B. Hoechst	1901-1910
Dr. Henry Kehm	1902-1909
Dr. Charles N. Wolf	1905-1907
Dr. Augustus G. Paetzel	-1908
Dr. Eugene Elgin	1909-1950
Dr. Robert Lau	1909-1915
Dr. Edgar A. Miller	1915-1923
Dr. A. W. Kelly	1934-1954
Dr. Roy Smith	1937-1944
Dr. Leon Roos	1946-
Dr. Joseph Eshleman	1950-

Dr. Wolf — Wife and son, Charles

Dr. H. B. Hoechst and wife, Mary.

Dr. Daniel L. Baker in his office.

Druggist: Charles S. Wolf 1890-1910

EAST BERLIN FAMILY MEDICINE is a medical office whose goal is to provide excellent, comprehensive, compassionate medical care to East Berlin and the surrounding communities. The office opened in September of 1983 when Michael E. Brown MD and Edward A. Nelson MD took over the practice of Leon Roos MD, a retiring general practitioner. The office at 337 West King Street was renovated and modernized. In January of 1994, the office was the first established practice to become part of the York Health System Medical group, which over time has become Wellspan Medical Group. In June of 1996, the office moved to 105 4th Street into a newly constructed building which houses the East Berlin Family Medicine, a Wellspan Lab and X-ray annex, and the Choice Apothecary.

The practice has grown significantly, expanding to 6 physicians and 1 physician assistant. This has allowed the office to provide medical care to over 10,000 patients in East Berlin and the surrounding area. A seventh physician will be added in August 2014. In order to continue to meet the needs of the population, there will be a satellite office opening in Cross Keys in September of 2014. We continue to strive to provide the highest quality care to the people we serve.

WALTERS CHIROPRACTIC

The office was first established in 1996. The practice began by renting space from Dr. Michael Zittle. They treated patients at that location for three years until the practice grew too large. Dr. Walters purchased the Victorian home located at 121 West King Street and renovated it, trying to preserve the historic style of the home. This is the present location in which they are serving the East Berlin Community by promoting health and wellness.

DENTISTS

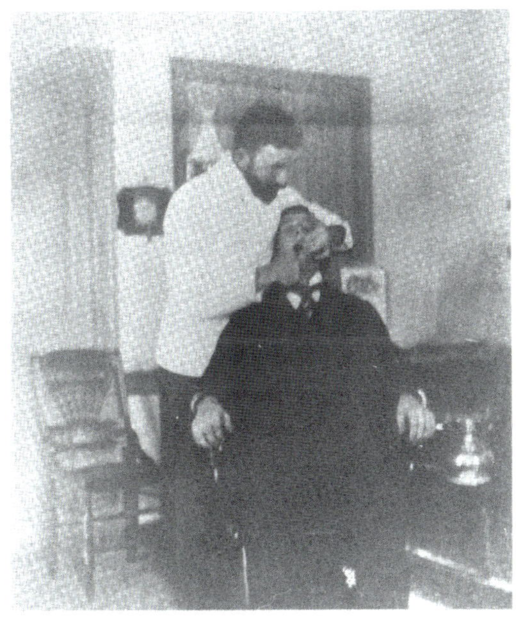

Dr. Elmer Lewis	
Dr. Robert Smith	1913-1914
Dr. A. W. Stinson	
Dr. Arthur Brewer	1940-1943
Dr. A. J. Hickey	1943-(8 mo.)
Dr. Robert J. Potts	1953

Dr. Elmer Lewis had his office in the house now owned by Miss Grace Stambaugh located three houses from Third Street on the north side of West King Street between Third and Fourth Street.

The picture on the left was taken in his office approximately seventy years ago.

OPTOMETRISTS

Rubin and Rubin	
Charles S. Wolf	1909-1917
Dr. A. W. Kelly	1940-1954
Dr. Joseph Eshelman	1952-1962
Dr. John Schwartz	1957-

VETERINARIANS

Dr. Robert Feiser
Dr. Edward Hudson
Dr. J. H. D. Bowersox

A diptheria epidemic in the town and surrounding area during the fall of 1901 claimed the lives of many of the children.

SHOPS

EAST BERLIN SMILES

418 West King Street

Todd Elgin, DMD, a lifelong resident of East Berlin, constructed the building at the current location, 418 West King St. in 1987. He began his practice, offering general and family dental services. He resided at the same address, in the apartment upstairs with his wife, Janice, his dental assistant. Dr. Elgin sold the practice and building to Lorena Cockley, DDS in 2002. Dr. Cockley continued the tradition of a high-quality care for which the practice was known and named it "East Berlin Smiles". There are 7 employees at the dental office currently.

DR. JOHN W. KLOPFER, D.D.S.

General and Family Dentistry

113 Harrisburg Street

Dr. Klopfer's dental practice originally started September 1983 in an office on Abbottstown Street, having purchased equipment from Dr. Arthur Breuer. In July 1987, Dr. Klopfer moved the practice to its current location at 113 Harrisburg Street after buying the building from retiring Dr. Robert Potts.

As the practice grew, many modifications and renovations have been completed, including the latest dental procedures and technology. Dr. Klopfer's dental practice has been recognized as one of the area's top dental practices by Harrisburg Magazine. Dr. Klopfer and his office staff are privileged to continue providing high-quality general and family dentistry to patients from East Berlin and its surrounding communities.

A Nineteenth Century Store

A. B. Mummert survived the sale.

Charles Spangler 1897-1920

Rudolph B. Glatfelter	1893-1900
C. M. Spahr	-1912
John Rider	1912-1938
Lau & Reynold	1917-1926
Charles & Lewis Spangler	1920-1930
Elmer Myers	1925-1929
David Kime	1930-
Lewis Spangler	1930-1949
Roy Mummert	1934-1946
George Moul	1937-1949
Stánton Debolt	1946-1952
Harold Gross	1947-1952
George Moul (Clothing)	1947-1960
Donald Moul	1952-1960
C. L. Spangler (Furniture)	1954-1956

HARDWARE STORES

On October 21, 1890 Noah Sprenkle purchased a lot in the center of town from Jacob Taughbaugh and started a Hardware business. Later, in 1915, he purchased a lot from Calvin Fohl on West King Street and moved his business to this location.

Daniel March operated a Hardware Store in 1911 in the building now occupied by the Peoples' State Bank on the Square.

Harry Sinner operated a Hardware Store on West King Street next to the Post Office; he was succeeded in this business operation by Mr. Weaver.

Curtis Spangler conducted a Hardware Store business for many years on the site now occupied by Glenn Cashman's Hardware Store.

NOTES OF INTEREST

About 1846, Cicero Stoner manufactured stoves which he sold along with tin ware. His business was located on East King Street in the home now owned by Paul March.

Horse-drawn carriages were sold by Calvin Fohl about the turn of the century on Harrisburg Street.

David Border, West King Street, sold farm machinery for a number of years.

William Spangler sold farm machinery for some years during the 1900's.

Daniel Guise sold buggies from the Edward Reynolds' shop for several years about 1912.

Myers and Mummert sold farm machinery on West King Street for several years.

W. F. Kuhn's Saddle Shop

Lewis Feiser also operated a saddle shop from 1910-1915 in the home now occupied by Arch Himes.

BAKE SHOPS

The first Bake Shop was located beside the David Border home. Later, another shop opened near the same location and was owned by Milton Brown. The bakers were Byron Lapham and Herman Wolf.

At a later date, Robert Shetter and Charles Wolf started a Bake Shop in the Red Man's Hall with Byron Lapham and Herman Wolf as bakers. Their line of baked goods included pretzels.

Clinton Cashman served a large part of the community with a bread route from 1915-1934; and, then, his son, Glenn, continued the business until 1942.

BUTCHERS

Charles Wolf	1890
Daniel Jacobs	
Robert Shetter	1897-1937
Bertus Eisenhart	1908-1947
Daniel Mummert	1915-1930
Jacob Grove	1923-1940
James Shaffer	1930
Orville Zeigler	

OTHER BUSINESSES

CREAMERY

A Creamery and two ice houses on the Conewago Creek east of Sixth Street were dismantled many years ago. Another creamery was built at the south end of Sixth Street. This building was destroyed in 1932 and was never rebuilt.

HOTELS AND RESTAURANTS

THE SUNDAY HOUSE

On June 19, 1884 William Sunday and his wife purchased two lots in East Berlin, No's 7 & 8, from Augustus Lerew and wife for a sum of $4600. This purchase included a brick house on a corner facing north on East King Street and west on the East-Berlin-Hanover Turnpike. On the site described here, the Sunday House was located.

Henry Sunday, a son, was hostler and part-time bartender. Meals were served for twenty-five cents.

William Sunday continued the business until 1916. Others who owned and operated the hotel were: a Ramer family, Ervin Hoover, John Hoover, Jack Anderson, and John Lehr.

THE SHAFFER HOUSE

The Shaffer House was located on the corner of West King Street and the East Berlin-Hanover Turnpike. The building was first constructed as a two-story building; and later (1890), Jacob Darone was employed to build a third floor to it to be used as a dance hall. The second floor had no halls or method of being heated, except for the "priest's room" which could be heated. This room was reserved for the visiting priests to the Paradise Catholic Church.

Robert Shetter removed the building when he built his home and butcher shop on the same site in 1920.

EISENHART HOTEL

Eisenhart's Hotel was a place of much activity following the Civil War. The Hotel was a regular over-night stop for cattle drovers.

During the nineteenth century, cattle and horses were driven on foot from Ohio and Virginia to markets in Lancaster County. The men were assisted by shepherding dogs. Twelve miles per day was the limit of an animal's endurance. At night, the animals were fed, watered and turned into a field on the farm of the Hotel.

The Hotel accommodated peddlers as well as travelers using the Conestoga wagons enroute between the Atlantic seaboard and areas west of the Allegheny Mountains. These travelers carried their own bedding; and when they found the Hotel crowded, they spread their bedding on the barroom floor and slept there.

George Eisenhart operated a tavern in the dwelling house on this farm from 1844 until 1873 at which time his son, George, Jr., assumed the business responsibilities and continued in operation until 1875.

Mr. and Mrs. Irvin Mummert now live on this farm. The house was rebuilt in 1907 on the original site of the Eisenhart Hotel.

RESTAURANT OWNERS

Frank Miller	
Harry Miller	
George Shetter	1924-1960
Melvin Boyer	
Robert Lau	1932-
Mervin Lau	1940-

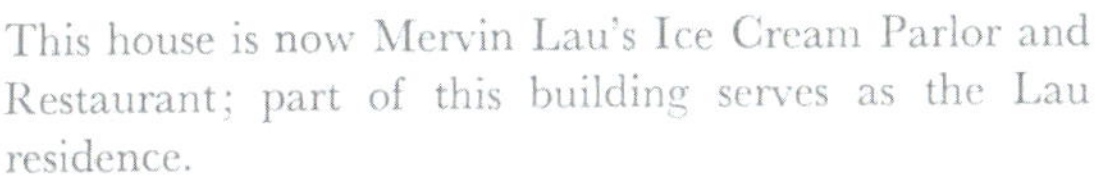

This house is now Mervin Lau's Ice Cream Parlor and Restaurant; part of this building serves as the Lau residence.

WAREHOUSES

On April 1, 1897 Noah Sprenkle purchased a lot on Locust Street from David and Clara March and built a Warehouse on this site. Curtis Leib operated this Warehouse until 1915 when Daniel Brandt bought the building to conduct a coal, feed and lumber business. Mr. Brandt operated the business until 1940 when his son, Verne Y. Brandt, took over the business. With the death of Verne Brandt in 1954, his son, Fred, continued its operation and is conducting business at the same location at present.

Denton Myers operated a feed, coal and lumber Warehouse on Locust Street from 1910 to 1946. This building was the train depot at one time. In 1947, John E. and Jesse Gentzler purchased the building and business and operated jointly until 1950 when Jesse took over independently. Jesse Gentzler is still in business at the same location today.

BLACKSMITHS

Lewis Bubb	1880
Noah Sell	1900
Frank Fissel	1910
Gilbert Haverstock	
John Jacobs	
Allen Philips	
Robert Philips	
Glayton Spahr	

This Blacksmith Shop is now being used by Ira Lobaugh for his lawn-mower service center.

GARAGES

Paul P. Lerew, 1917-1954: Started on Abbottstown Street, associated with Cleason Smith; later moved to Harrisburg Street.

As business improved, expansion became necessary. In 1947, the business became Lerew's, Incorporated.

GARAGE OWNERS

William Mummert	1915	Ralph Boyer	1947-1962
Lewis Feiser	1915-1919	Mervin Chronister	1956-
George Mummert	1919-1958	Elmer Mummert	1958
William Ruth	1920-1940	East Berlin Garage:	1960-
Cletus Mummert	1936	(Richard Smyers and Paul Fahs, owners)	
George Glatfelter	1936-1956		

TRUCKING

MILK ROUTE

In 1916, John Myers of East Berlin established a milk route between East Berlin and York. Milk was secured from farms of this community and sold to the York Sanitary Milk Company. The trip was made daily with a team of horses and wagon. He also took orders from merchants of East Berlin and Abbottstown, and on the return trip, delivered the merchandise.

In 1917, Mr. Myers purchased his first truck, and business expanded rapidly.

A heavy snowfall during the winter of 1918 created many delays in travel, including the trucking business. Mr. Myers started his daily trip at eight o'clock one morning and did not return for twenty-six hours. He became stranded on the Thomasville hill and hired twenty men to shovel a roadway on both sides of the hill in order for him to continue his trip.

Mr. Myers operated three trucks for ten years hauling baled hay to the railroad depot for shipment, grain to the mill and warehouses and "flittens" for people in the community.

In 1939, he sold his business to Joseph Altland of Paradise Township, York County.

MUMMERT'S TRANSFER

Cletus Mummert, owner of the Mummert Transfer Company, began from "scratch" in 1932 with a Model "A" Ford Truck. His first base of operation was in the barn of his residence on West King Street. Needing more space, he moved his business in 1937 to the property formerly occupied by several shoe factories on West King Street. He also contracted school buses to the local school district for many years. Today, his many trucks can be seen traveling over the eastern section of the United States.

JOHN T. PHILIPS, HAULING

Mr. Philips purchased his first truck in 1936 and commenced hauling building and construction stone. In 1939, he purchased a new truck and started hauling stone and lime for the Thomasville Stone and Lime Company. Mr. Philips started spreading lime with an automatic lime spreader in 1942 and has hauled materials from the many quarries of York, Adams, and Cumberland Counties. He also does hauling for the State Highway Department on a contract basis.

1964 Original Pages

PLUMBERS

Jacob Resser, immediately following his discharge from serving in the Civil War in 1865, founded the tin-shop business in East Berlin. He continued this business until 1889, when he turned it over to his son, Walter. Walter operated the business until 1903 and then sold it to his brother, William, who managed the business until his death in 1941.

The business, however, was not always located at the same site. Following Mrs. Jacob Resser's death in 1920, the old homestead was sold; and William W. Resser was forced to vacate the place. Therefore, he erected a new shop a short distance east, adjacent to his home; and from this point, he conducted his business.

John Butt	1910
Samuel Kling	1913-1940
Lewis Smith	1924-1945
Justin Resser	1945
Smith & Eisenhart	1945-1951
Sheffers	1947-
Lynn Slothour	1950-1962
James Eisenhart	1951-
Stewart Miller	1954-
Horace Baker	1962-

HUCKSTERS

The *huckster* was an institution, a cog in the wheel that brought our country from the pioneer's log cabin to greatness.

The *huckster wagon,* which at one time linked the American farms to the village stores, belongs to the past along with the buggy, the buffalo robe and the horsedrawn wagon.

Through heat, cold, rain, snow, storm, and over the roughest roads, he made his rounds in his canvas-covered wagon.

The late Martin D. Wentz operated one of the last of these horse-drawn, huckster routes; for approximately twenty years, Mr. Wentz was engaged in this business. From about 1910 to 1930, his canvas-topped wagon was drawn by two heavy bay Belgian horses, Maudie and Frank.

He bought country produce such as butter, eggs, poultry from the farmers in the surrounding community. Eggs were carried in crates and poultry in "coops" hung beneath the "tailgate" of the wagon.

The shelves of his wagon carried staples such as sugar, coffee, salt, rice, flour, corn meal, and also tobacco.

In real cold weather, he used a small charcoal-burning foot warmer.

Jane Wisler made hair switches in the early 1900's and lived in what was later the Carmon Myers' home.

Mrs. Rosa Gladfelter had the Bell Telephone Exchange in her home from 1914-1921. Members of her family assisted her.

Mrs. Herman (Sally) Wolf operated the York Telephone Exchange in her home for 38 years, from 1916-1954. Her assistants were Miss Bertha Hull and Mrs. Sherman Krall. Sally is pictured here.

#1073. W. Main St. from Square, East Berlin, Pa.

Square, East Berlin, Pa.

1964 Original Pages

GYPSIES

Many of us remember the basket makers, bands of gypsies, who often made their appearance along the streams of our community. They would make and sell baskets, tell fortunes and trade or steal horses. Usually, they stayed around until someone who had been cheated took them to a "squire's" office to be ordered out of the area. They visited and traded in this area as late as 1909.

. . . AND MANY OTHERS

Wool and linen coverlets were made nearby about 1838 to 1860 by Martin B. Brenneman. In two corners of each coverlet were woven the name of the person for whom it was made and the year in which it was made. Some residents of East Berlin still own some of these coverlets . . . Emanuel Kuhn was a "cooper" (barrel maker) by trade in the 1840's . . . Samuel Miller molded pottery from about 1865 to 1903. Some articles of this pottery can still be found in the community . . . Moses Sclar operated a Junk Yard on West King Street in 1912 . . . Mrs. Lewis Border, Elizabeth Swartz, Maude Myers, Esther Deihl and Mrs. William Ruth were some of the milliners in the town . . . Herman Wolf's Shoe Repair Shop was first located near the Elementary School but later moved to his home on Fourth Street. He was in the shoe-repair business from 1925-1952.

THE BUSINESSES OF TODAY

APPLIANCES
Roy Boyer
Home Service & Supply
Kunkle's Appliances
BANKS
East Berlin National Bank
Peoples' State Bank of East Berlin
BARBERS
Lavere Burgard
Earl Zeigler
BEAUTY SHOPS
Evelyn Eisenhart
Jeanne's Beauty Shop
BUTCHER
Nell's Slaughter House
DRY CLEANERS
Smith's Dry Cleaning
Larry's Dry Cleaning
ELECTRICIANS
Elmer Leas
Roy Boyer
FACTORIES
Gettysburg Shoe Company
East Berlin Garment Co.
Penn Wood Products
Beau Products, Inc.
GARAGES
East Berlin Garage
Chronister's Garage
Krout's Garage
Lerew's Incorporated
GROCERS
Robert Lau — Cut Rate Variety
Mrs. Herbert Myers
Nell's Food Market
HARDWARE
Glenn Cashman

INSURANCE & REAL ESTATE
John Baker
Danner
Charles Graybill
Archie Himes
Pauline Kunkle
Harper Philips
MILLS
Brandt Feed & Lumber
East Berlin Milling Company
Eisenhart's Mill
Gentzler Feed & Lumber
MORTICIAN
Richard Emig
PAINTERS
Guerney Alwine
Roy & Lester Chronister
Glenn Herman
George Zeigler
PLUMBERS
Horace Baker
James Eisenhart
Stewart Miller
PRINTER
Altland's Print Shop
RESTAURANTS
Lau's Restaurant
Mervin Lau
Sam's Place
ROOFER
Glenn Herman
OTHERS
Grizzell's Gun Shop
Glatfelter's Surge Dairy Equipment
Lobaugh's Lawn Mower Sales & Svc.
East Berlin Laundromat

LABORATORY, ANALYTICAL & BIOLOGICAL SERVICES, INC.

(LABS, Inc.) is owned and operated by President, Fred S. Richstien II and Vice President, Fred S. Richstien Sr. LABS, Inc. has been providing municipal, commercial, industrial, and residential clients with quality service since 1996.

LABS, Inc. is a Pennsylvania Department of Environmental Protection (PADEP #01-550) and Maryland Department of the Environment (MD #300) certified laboratory that specializes in water quality parameters and environmental testing. Employees have the extensive training and technical background necessary to address water treatment problems and their solutions. The lab is happy to assist all individuals, from home-owners to operators.

Mission Statement:

LABS, Inc. realizes that our customers require reproducible, legally defensible, and expedient laboratory results, and is dedicated to providing clients with the highest-quality service.

We provide clients with cost-effective analytical solutions to meet their needs and exceed their expectations. Superior customer service, scientifically sound analytical data, and our customer's regulatory compliance are our highest priorities.

TUCKER INDUSTRIAL LIQUID COATINGS

March 2013 marked the 20th anniversary for Tucker Industrial Liquid Coatings, an in-demand company specializing in high-tech surface finishing services for military, commercial, and industrial applications. Founded by Bernie Tucker with one employee in 1993, Tucker now occupies more than 60,000 square feet of space and employs more than 35 people. Tucker attributes his success to close partnerships with clients, high quality standards and dedicated employees.

THE ZEIGLER FEED MILL

The mill has been an institution in East Berlin for many years. The current site on West King St. was originally developed as a feed and flour mill by Noah Sell in the late 1800s. Mr. Sell, the great, great-grandfather of the current company owners, was one of the founders of the first bank in East Berlin. The mill property was transferred from Round Hill Foods, Inc. to the Zeigler organization in 1984 and underwent significant renovations ten years later.

Zeigler Bros., Inc, which is now owned and managed by the third generation (Tim and Matt Zeigler) was founded in 1935 when the brothers Ty and Le Roy Zeigler purchased a water-powered gristmill along the Conewago Creek between Arendtsville and Biglerville. The company grew steadily and today employs about 70 employees, with more than half working at the East Berlin facility while the corporate offices are located in Gardners.

The business started out as a simple feed mill servicing Adams County dairy and chicken farms. It is now a technological, innovative global leader making feeds for fish, shrimp, exotic pets, birds, reptiles, and zoo animals. Zeigler's also produces feeds for laboratory animals used in biomedical research, mixing old and new technology.

Through the years, the company has experienced various business cycles filled with many successes, but many hard times as well, such as fires, economic recessions and failed markets. However, the company remains stable and continues to grow which is a testimonial and tribute to the fine Zeigler Team.

Dr. Tom Zeigler (second generation) and his wife Freda are proud of their Adams County background and have contributed to the community in many ways, such as first president of the upper Adams Jaycees and they helped organize the first Apple Harvest Festival. The use of the large lot behind the East Berlin mill has been donated for use by the community sports teams.

Some of Zeigler's notable contributions and fun facts are providing nutritional support for the Panda bears gifted to President Nixon by the Chinese government they also supplied a complete diet in liquid form for rodents to be used in space exploration. If you are a Pennsylvania trout fisherman (or woman), most likely the fish you catch were hatched in a state hatchery and fed with Zeigler trout feed.

Today, continuing as a family-owned organization, Zeigler sells its products in about 45 of the U.S. states and exports to around 50 countries. Exports account for approximately 50% of the company's sales. In addition, Zeigler aquaculture products are produced in several other countries under licensing and technology transfer agreements.

EAST BERLIN AREA JOINT AUTHORITY

As far back as 2001, discussions began on the anticipated end-of-life of the old sewer plant, and the need to replace it. At first, no expansion of the sewer plant beyond the Borough's needs were considered. Then discussions lay dormant for a few years.

When C.W. Test bought the Buttercup Farm for development on the outskirts of the town, C.W. Test and Hamilton Township supervisors approached the Borough Council in October of 2004 to possibly supply the sewer needs for the proposed development. This created a lot of discussions over a long period of time. During the discussions with Hamilton Township Supervisors the Borough learned Hamilton Township's preference of using a joint authority to handle the situation, because they did not want to operate a sewer and water system.

The East Berlin Borough Council under the advice of legal council unanimously approved an agreement with C.W. Test on December 6, 2006. The East Berlin Borough Council and the Hamilton Township Supervisors signed Intermunicipal Agreements and Resolutions and thus the East Berlin Area Joint Authority was created pursuant to the Municipal Authorities Act, 53 Pa.c.s.§5601 as amended. On October 15, 2007, the Articles of Incorporation were filed with the State of Pennsylvania and the East Berlin Area Joint Authority became an official Authority. At that point, the Borough and the Authority became two separate entities. The Authority is responsible for the administration and operation of the water system and sewer system including the construction, maintenance and rate-making. The organizational meeting of the East Berlin Area Joint Authority was held on November 1, 2007; at 7:00 PM; at the East Berlin Borough office at 128 Water Street.

The appointments to the East Berlin Area Joint Authority were staggered with 1 to 5 year terms. The East Berlin Borough Council appointed 4 members; 3 were from the water and sewer committee of the Borough Council and one private citizen. The 5th member was appointed by Hamilton Township. The first appointed board members from the Borough were Charles M. Eisenhart for one year, Gregery Green for two years, John Lerew for three years, Gerald L. Mummert for four years, and from Hamilton

Township, John C. O'Brien for five years. The East Berlin Area Joint Authority Board members were not compensated for their efforts and hard work to maintain and operate the Authority; and, to date, are still not compensated. The East Berlin Area Joint Authority held their monthly meetings the first Thursday of each month at 7 PM at the Borough Hall. The Authority has since relocated their office to 103 Locust Street.

SEWER SYSTEM

The Authority proceeded with the required planning and approval processes for the expansion of the new state-of-the-art sewer plant. The plans also included other improvements to the sewer network and the connection for the C.W. Test development. The Authority entered into this agreement due to the financial benefits to the Borough. C.W. Test's participation would account for approximately 60% of the projected cost for the sewer plant. Along with the sewer project cost benefits, substantial water resources were deeded to the East Berlin Area Joint Authority by the Buttercup Farm developer. So when, the Buttercup Farm property is finally developed, they will be using East Berlin Area Joint Authority facilities and contributing to the water resources.

Bids were requested in 2008, but due to economic conditions, bids were higher than expected, and C.W. Test was not able to obtain financing for their portion of the project; thus ending their participation in the project. The citizens of the East Berlin Borough would have been in debt for over eight million dollars if it wasn't for the planning of the past Borough Council working with the Buttercup Farms developer-C.W. Test.

On January 5, 2009, representatives from Representative Will Tallman's office, Senator Rich Alloway's office, the Department of Environmental Protection, PennVest and Reading Township met with the East Berlin Area Joint Authority Board and their engineers-Buchart-Horn, Inc. to discuss funding for replacement of the East Berlin sewer plant, based on Department of Environmental Protection and Susquehanna River Basin Commission requirements. The outcome of that meeting determined that the project was favorable for funding by the Department of Environmental Protection and PennVest because of its regional nature and immediate need. The proposed sewer plant would serve the Buttercup Farm area of Hamilton Township and the Borough of East Berlin.

On October 1, 2009, the papers were signed for a loan of $4,153,407.00 and a grant for $3,950,000.00 for a total expense of the new sewer treatment plant of $8,103,407.00.

On October 2, 2009 at 1:00 p.m., the groundbreaking ceremony was held for the new state-of-the-art wastewater treatment plant. State Senator Rich Alloway was the guest speaker at the ceremony.

The project was given 14 months to complete. In addition to the construction of the new sewer plant; the project also involved demolition of the old sewer plant in the same area and the small pumping station on the west side of town. New sewer piping was laid on Water Street, and new water and sewer service was installed to nine properties on Schoolhouse Lane, which previously had wells and on-lot sewer systems.

The new wastewater treatment plant was designed by Buchart-Horn, Inc. and was built by Johnston Construction Company, the electrical work was done by Garden Spot Electric, Inc. and Gregory Contractors laid the piping for the sewer lines.

The new wastewater treatment plant was subsequently completed in December 2010.

The ribbon cutting ceremony was held April 14, 2011 to celebrate the opening of the wastewater treatment plant.

This new treatment plant uses biological nutrient removal technology and a sequencing batch reactor process to remove nitrogen and phosphorus from the sewage to meet the PA Department of Environmental Protection's standards as part of the Chesapeake Bay Tributary strategy. This new system will not only clean wastewater better but also reduces the energy cost of operating the system.

WATER SYSTEM

East Berlin's original water system was installed in 1896, and much of the original cast iron piping still remains. The early utility piping was installed in the two state roads that cross the Borough; they are Route 234 (King Street) and Route 194 (Abbottstown Street and Harrisburg Street).

The East Berlin Area Joint Authority's drinking water is supplied from four wells and stored in two elevated storage tanks. The Authority is currently working on getting a fifth well up and running. This well is located outside of town off of Route 194, on the farm behind Nell's Shurfine grocery store.

The Authority maintains the fire hydrants in the Borough and is continually checking and maintaining the upkeep on them. The Authority will be installing isolation valves for the hydrants. Occasionally, some of the hydrants are replaced, to ensure they are in proper working order.

The East Berlin Area Joint Authority's Capital Improvement Plan for the upcoming years is to replace old asbestos cement piping in the water system, replace old water mains, some of which are over 100 years old and under-sized, replace 50 year old elevated storage tank to increase the storage capacity, and replace outdated telemetry for well and tank controls.

The Authority monitors and sends out an annual report of the previous year water quality, required by the Department of Environmental Protection, usually with your April billing. This report states the test results and the limits for the chemicals and possible contaminants in the water system.

In the last two years, the Authority has started replacing the old water meters with automatic radio reading meters. This will eventually replace the existing card system, which in turn, will reduce postage expense.

The employees of the East Berlin Area Joint Authority work very hard on a daily basis to provide top quality water to your tap. Our constant goal is to provide our customers with a quality and dependable supply of drinking water. We ask that all our customers help us protect our water resources, which are the heart of our community, our way of life, and our children's future.

EAST BERLIN BEVERAGE DISTRIBUTORS INC.

In 1956, Cletus E. Mummert started the Cletus Mummert Beer Distributor in East Berlin. At that time, the Beer Distributor was located at the rear of 312 W. King St., about ½ block west of its current location. On November 22, 1963, Robert and Beverly Eichelberger purchased the Beer Distributor from Cletus Mummert. They changed the name to East Berlin Beverage Distributors, and a legacy was born. In July of 1973, Robert and Beverly incorporated the business, which then became East Berlin Beverage Dist., Inc. The officers and shareholders of the newly formed corporation were Robert A. Eichelberger, President; Harry L. Eichelberger, Vice President; Beverly Eichelberger, Secretary/Treasurer; Grace Eichelberger, stockholder.

In 1975, Cletus Mummert passed away and the building that housed East Berlin Beverage Dist. Inc., was sold. The Eichelbergers purchased the property at the corner of W. King and 3rd Street where they built the "new" warehouse, which is the site of the current business. Sadly, on September 20, 1978, Beverly Eichelberger was killed in a car accident. On October 3, 1980, Robert and Beverly's daughter, Roberta (Robbie) J. Teal was elected to the board as Secretary/Treasurer. She remained in that position until the passing of her father, Robert, in April 2004, at which time, she became the acting President. Robbie purchased the business and property from the estate on December 20, 2004, and continued in the business until this day. On November 22, 2013, East Berlin Beverage Dist., Inc. celebrated its 50th year in business.

THOMASON'S HERB FARM & GIFT SHOP

Opened in September 1997. They started the business in a 15 x 20 room in their house. They have now expanded to a salt-box style house, while also occupying an old milk house. Who knows what they will get into next.

They sell plants (herbs & flowers) in the spring. The gift shop is loaded with jewelry, purses, scarves, pottery, home-made soap, antiques, loose tea, tea items and much more. The garden shed has bee skeps, garden markers, chimes, bird feeders, fairy garden items, etc. If you hang around long enough, you might even hear a tall-tale or some bluegrass music.

COMPUTER REPAIRS AND SERVICES

Computer Marketing Technologies

418 West King Street

Joshua Cockley moved his computer business to East Berlin in July 2005. Josh began CMTech in Hanover in 1996 at the age of 14 years. He currently services and repairs computers on-site and in his computer repair shop which was the former apartment and home of Dr. and Mrs. Todd Elgin. Josh currently has 3 employees and is an expert in repairing, designing and networking computer systems for homes and businesses.

COUNTRY HEARTH FLOWER & GIFT SHOP

Country Hearth Flower & Gift Shop opened on April 1, 1993. People said a flower and gift shop can't make it in East Berlin. So, appropriately we picked April Fool's Day to give it a try.

With lots of hard work, long hours and determination, we are still here! Country Hearth is a full-service flower shop serving the East Berlin area and surrounding communities. Stephanie (Thomas) Stoltzfus is Owner, Manager and Floral Designer. On holidays, you can find as many as 10 temporary employees helping out at the shop. We are located at 309 West King Street in the big yellow building with the ivy growing around the sign post.

BECHTEL VICTORIAN MANSION BED & BREAKFAST

400 West King Street | East Berlin, PA 17316
(717) 259-7760
www.bechtelvictorianmansion.com

The Bechtal Victorian Mansion Bed & Breakfast is located at 400 West King Street in East Berlin. The largest home in town, it was built for the family of William G. Leas in 1897. Mr. Leas was a prominent entrepreneur/businessman at the turn of the 19th century. The home remained with the Leas family for 85 years and was then sold at auction to Charles and Mariam Bechtel in 1982. The Bechtels had extensive work done on the house before they opened a bed and breakfast in 1983. The Inn originally featured 6 guestrooms. Further renovations added 3 more guestrooms on the third floor. Local resident Ruth Spangler served as Innkeeper, along with the Bechtels.

In 1999, the home was sold to Richard and Carol Carlson, originally from Connecticut. The Carlsons had been searching for a bed and breakfast for over two years before they fell in love with this house. Immediately, they began redecorating each of the Inn's 9 bedrooms, 3 parlors, and 9 guest bathrooms. A new kitchen was installed in the defunct original one, and the pantry was returned to its former use. The extensive work includes adding period wallpapers, Victorian picture rails and ceiling medallions, all while preserving the integrity of the home's beautiful woodwork, windows, and built-ins. All rooms are furnished with a combination of period antiques and comfortable newer pieces, in a country Victorian style.

The Carlsons have operated the bed and breakfast since April, 1999. They have moved their living quarters to the third floor and run the six guest-room Inn year round. The six rooms include two suites, each room with private bath. Guests are treated to homemade cookies or other treats upon arrival; and everyone enjoys a delicious homemade breakfast each morning, which consists of fresh fruit, homemade breads, muffins, or scones, and a hot dish, such as our oven-baked orange french toast, a guest favorite. An endless supply of coffee, tea, and juice are also served.

Adams County National Bank	1677 Rt. 194 North	East Berlin Pa 17316	334-3161
Allen Woodworking	Rear 511 West King Street	East Berlin Pa 17316	624-9011
Applachian Reality Co	PO Box 180	East Berlin Pa 17316	259-9551
Apple Valley Creamery LLC	541 Germany Road	East Berlin Pa 17316	528-4520
Bechtel Victorian Mansion B & B Inn	400 W. King St	East Berlin Pa 17316	259-7760
Beverly Jadus Antiques	541 W. King St	East Berlin Pa 17316	259-7049
Cashman's True Value	1595 Rt. 194 North	East Berlin Pa 17316	259-0922
Catherine's Hair Replacement Center	105 W. King Street	East Berlin Pa 17316	259-0085
Choice Apothecary	105 Fourth Street	East Berlin Pa 17316	259-6440
CGA Law Firm	PO Box 606, 106 Harrisburg St	East Berlin Pa 17316	259-9592
Computer Marketing Technologies	418 W. King Street	East Berlin Pa 17316	259-8980
Country Hearth Flower & Gift Shop	309 W. King St	East Berlin Pa 17316	259-7572
Curves	401 W. King St.	East Berlin Pa 17316	259-6790
Danner's Insurance	401 Abbottstown St	East Berlin Pa 17316	259-7122
Dylan's Bar And Restaurant	321 Harrisburg St	East Berlin Pa 17316	259-0212
East Berlin Beverage Dist., Inc	PO Box 171, W. King St	East Berlin Pa 17316	259-0513
East Berlin Car Wash	406 Abbottstown St	East Berlin Pa 17316	259-8755
East Berlin Chiropractor	337 W. King St	East Berlin Pa 17316	259-8813
East Berlin Community Center	405 North Ave	East Berlin Pa 17316	259-8848
East Berlin Community Library	105 Locust St	East Berlin Pa 17316	259-9000
East Berlin Excavating, Inc.	531 W. King St	East Berlin Pa 17316	259-9071
East Berlin Family Care Center	312 Harrisburg St	East Berlin Pa 17316	259-0222
East Berlin Family Medicine	105 4th Street	East Berlin Pa 17316	259-9568
East Berlin Family Restaurant	130 W. King Street	East Berlin Pa 17316	619-7008
East Berlin Fitness Center	405 North Ave	East Berlin Pa 17316	259-0149
East Berlin Fire Company	E. Locust St	East Berlin Pa 17316	259-7125
East Berlin Foot & Ankle Center	201 Harrisburg St	East Berlin Pa 17316	259-8637
East Berlin Historical Preservation Society	PO Box 73, 332 W. King St	East Berlin Pa 17316	259-0822

East Berlin Pharmacy	PO Box 1013, 335 W. King St	East Berlin Pa 17316	259-0421
East Berlin Senior Center	405 North Ave	East Berlin Pa 17316	259-9630
Feiser Funeral Home	306 Harrisburg St	East Berlin Pa 17316	259-7131
Frick Company	405 W. King St	East Berlin Pa 17316	259-9755
H & R Block	106 Abbottstown St	East Berlin Pa 17316	259-9469
Hoffman & Woodward Makers	412 W. King St	East Berlin Pa 17316	259-7676
Hog Wild Catering and BBQ Carry Out	507 W. King St.	East Berlin Pa 17316	259-6203
Jim & Nena's Pizzeria	112 Abbottstown St	East Berlin Pa 17316	259-8496
John Klopfer, D.D.S.	PO Box 648, 113 Harrisburg St	East Berlin Pa 17316	259-9612
Kathy's Carousel Of Dance	511 W. King St	East Berlin Pa 17316	259-1045
L & L Ford	314 Harrisburg St	East Berlin Pa 17316	259-6334
L.A.B.S.	409 North Ave	East Berlin Pa 17316	259-6550
Lion & The Lamb	548 W. King St	East Berlin Pa 17316	259-9866
Lorena Cockley, D.D.S.	418 W. King St	East Berlin Pa 17316	259-9596
Madison Bay	PO Box 656	East Berlin Pa 17316	259-6886
Mason Propane Service	PO Box 1012, 317 W. King St	East Berlin Pa 17316	259-0624
Michelangelo's Hair Studio, Inc	209 Locust St	East Berlin Pa 17316	259-9310
Nell's Shurfine Market	30 Primrose Lane	East Berlin Pa 17316	259-4868
Old Glory Salon	209 Locust St	East Berlin Pa 17316	259-0233
Omy, Inc	312 Harrisburg St	East Berlin Pa 17316	259-0718
OTI: Orbit Technologies Inc.	209 Locust St	East Berlin Pa 17316	619-7163
Paul A. Grim Stone Masonry Inc.	340 Beavercreek Rd	East Berlin Pa 17316	259-7888
Pennwood Products	PO Box 180	East Berlin Pa 17316	259-9551
Rocco's Pizza	500 W. King St	East Berlin Pa 17316	259-7287
Rutter's Farm Store 99	Abbottstown St	East Berlin Pa 17316	259-7926
Sidney Restaurant	PO Box 557, 101 E. King St	East Berlin Pa 17316	259-1319
Sneed's Antiques	409 W. King St	East Berlin Pa 17316	259-8275
Subway	415 Abbottstown St	East Berlin Pa 17316	259-8200
Susquehanna Bank	100 E. King St	East Berlin Pa 17316	259-2516
Tackroom Treasures	424 Abbottstown St	East Berlin Pa 17316	259-0571
Tail Chasers	501 W. King Street	East Berlin Pa 17316	259-7024
Thomason's Herb Farm & Gift Shop	170 Stoney Point Rd.	East Berlin Pa 17316	624-1527
Tucker Industries	407 North Ave	East Berlin Pa 17316	259-8339
V.F.W. Post 8896	Locust St	East Berlin Pa 17316	259-0124
Walter's Chiropractic	121 W. King St	East Berlin Pa 17316	259-8056
Wayne Nell and Sons Meats	2218 Baltimore Pike	East Berlin Pa 17316	259-9587
Wayne's Shoe Repair	400 Abbottstown St	East Berlin Pa 17316	259-0266
White Dove Laundramat	112 Abbottstown St	East Berlin Pa 17316	
Woolgatherings	529 W. King St	East Berlin Pa 17316	259-0924
Zeigler's Barber Shop	120 W. King St	East Berlin Pa 17316	259-9324
Zeigler Bros., Inc.	619 W. King St	East Berlin Pa 17316	259-9461
Zwingli's Christian School	403 W. King St	East Berlin Pa 17316	259-7449

TRANSPORTATION

TRANSPORTATION

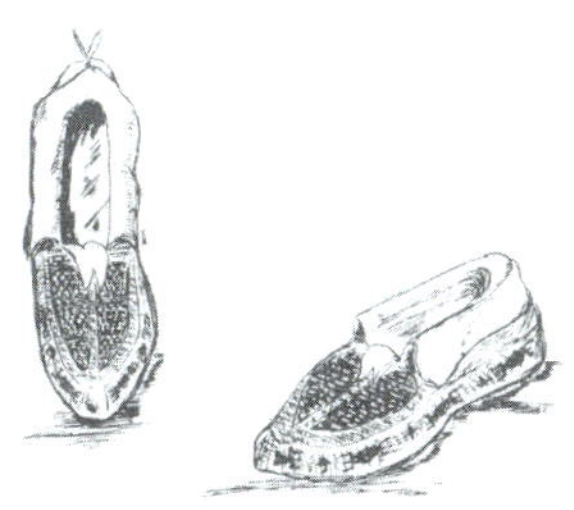

On the sandy and muddy banks of the Conewago, through the tall and unrestrained grasslands, and into the surrounding wooded areas, man's first mode of transportation in our community was revealed by the light indents of the soft, deer-skin moccasin. Sometimes these prints came to an abrupt halt at the edge of the stream; further along the stream, the banks showed that the early inhabitants continued their journeys. Man's earliest means of waterway transportation was evidenced by the carefully hollowed logs found nearby.

When the *white man* moved into this area, *his* mode of transportation was indicated by a different set of tracks — those of the "hobnail boots" followed by the hoofprints of the pack horse.

Shortly after the arrival of the early settlers, one of man's greatest inventions — the wheel — began to leave its tracks in the areas where the trails were widened and made passable for the contrivance attached to the wheel. The wagon, with its many varied shapes and forms and designed for the needs and purposes of the individual, became the main mode of transportation. The wagon was often used as a shelter, until a temporary home could be built. After the land was cleared and the permanent log cabin was constructed, the wagon's primary usage was that of transporting the needs of the settler and his family.

Many years elapsed before the settlers had anything to sell; therefore, they had little with which to buy supplies. The first "dry goods" were brought to the locality by the itinerant peddler. The pack-laden peddler was one of the valued institutions of the area. His visits were few and far between, but an annual visit was sufficient to supply most of the demands for his wares.

The Indian trails became wider and eventually turned into "dirt roads"; in the Spring and Fall, these were called "mud roads," in keeping with their condition. The "dirt roads" criss-crossed through the entire vicinity, and certain of these were traveled more heavily than others. Where two such roads crossed, a site or a town was established. And in such a manner, came the development of *Berlin*.

The residents of the early decades of the nineteenth century witnessed the commencement of a road-building program. About 1810, people living in Adams and York Counties began agitating for hard-surfaced roads, which were then called *turnpikes*. This brought about the formation of the Berlin-Hanover Turnpike Company, which was incorporated by an Act of Assembly of the Commonwealth in 1810. The Act of Incorporation named the following persons as commissioners: Samuel Fahnestock, Boreus Fahnestock, John B. Arnold, William Patterson, Tobias Kepner and Frederick Baugher. Samuel Fahnestock was elected President at a Board of Directors' meeting on December 11, 1811.

The base of the turnpike consisted of fairly large stones upon which successive layers of smaller stones were placed. As the top layer deteriorated by reason of hard usage and weather conditions, it was replaced. This was the type of construction used on the Berlin-Hanover Turnpike, a distance of ten miles and the first hard-surfaced road to enter town. Distances of this type turnpike were indicated by "milestones," usually placed at intervals of one mile. Several of these stones are still intact and can be seen along this road. Two — later three — tollgates were placed on the turnpike, and a toll-gate keeper was stationed at each to collect tolls from persons using the pike. One gate was removed from its original site and re-established to "catch" people who branched off the nearest road to reach their destination without paying toll. The gate first removed, known as the Hamilton Gate House, is located at the south edge of town.

The existence of the Conewago Creek was another important factor responsible for the development of *Berlin* at *this* particular location. Even though the Creek provided great assistance to the early residents, it was also a hindrance when the waters raised to high levels causing the fords to become impassable. As the settler progressed, this problem was overcome through the construction of bridges.

What was more majestic to the American scene than the covered bridge? Here was American architecture and construction reminiscent of Colonial intuitiveness. Here was an escape, a refuge for the traveler from the cold northern winds and snow of the wintry day; here was a safe and comfortable respite before continuing on his journey. Who could count the number of times such a structure saved the passerby from the sound soaking of a sudden summer shower, or the times it gave a cooling effect from the hot summer sun as he strayed under its sturdy roof. Even beneath it, the fisherman could sit in a downpour and fish to his heart's content with no fear of being drenched. How often could one find a winter sports' enthusiast building a fire on the ice, seeking protection from one of the graceful piers? Not only man, but birds and animals saw its protective value from the cold winds and rain. And most of all, what safer way was there of crossing winter's half-frozen streams or the torrent creeks of spring?

As time progresses and brings to us many modern advantages, it also takes from us the by-gone necessities that were also beautiful and pleasurable. Be thankful if you can reminisce about this, our majestic American scene.

Mummert's Grove Bridge

Picture of the Kuhn Fording Bridge painted by Ursula Martino

KUHN FORDING BRIDGE

(formerly Mummert's Grove Bridge)

In 1972, Hurricane Agnes came through the area causing high flood water, as the town is all but surrounded by the Conewago Creek. Then again in September 1975, the town was hit by Hurricane Eloise, causing extensive property damage to the East Berlin area including the loss of the Kuhn Fording Covered Bridge. The tragic loss of the historic landmark was deeply felt by the citizens of the community.

An ad-hoc committee was formed by the East Berlin Historic Preservation Society to initiate a campaign to restore the bridge, as it was one of the longest covered bridges in the state.

After much work by the committee, funding by the Federal government was in place. Court battles with the County officials were won over rebuilding the bridge.

The County Commissioners were planning to sell the bridge rather than restore it. The first phase of reconstruction was started. The contract was awarded to Stephen Esh, a Lancaster barn builder, and Glen Crouse, as Littlestown heavy equipment operator.

On January 14, 1976, tragedy struck as Esh and Crouse went upstream in search of missing timbers from the bridge. Their boat capsized and came back downstream empty. Over 200 people searched for two days before recovering the bodies of the two drowned men.

The saga of the Kuhn Fording Bridge continued for two more years before it was put to rest along with Steve Esh and Glen Crouse. The remainder of the bridge timbers were given to Lancaster County to be used to repair of their cherished covered bridges.

Kuhn Fording Bridge

Lyrics Oscar F. Spicer, Music Bruce R. VanDyke

In eastern Adams County a covered bridge does stand
A witness to an era when things were made by hand
But time has not dealt kindly, its appearance makes so plain
Say those who run the county, too costly to maintain

A hurricane one autumn assailed it where it stood
Vowed those around who loved it, to fix it if they could
Beneath that covered structure the Conewago flows
And in its wintry waters, dark tragedy arose.

Chorus
Oh Kuhn's Fording Bridge, you made your builders proud
Will you like they vanish into yesterday
How much time are you allowed?

A builder and a plain man were working with a crew,
They rowed a small boat upstream to get a better view
The time was February, what happened never learned
But those two brave souls perished, their small boat overturned

(Chorus)

You'd think we would remember the sacrifice they made
And strive to save that structure for which they dearly paid
But like the Conewago we rush along our way
We have no time or patience for things of yesterday

(Altered Chorus)
Oh Kuhn's Fording Bridge, what time are you allowed?
Oh cold Conewago, your waters were a shroud

For our Sunday afternoon ride, we headed west.

We approached the double covered bridge . . .

. . . and stopped for a side view.

Then, we entered the bridge . . .

. . . upon leaving the bridge, we glanced back.

In 1821, a seven-arch stone bridge which was 213 feet long, was constructed at what was then known as Geiselman's Mill at a cost of $5000. This bridge stood for just a few years when an ice jam broke, and the resulting flood damaged it severly. It was then replaced in 1826 by a three-span, wooden, double-covered bridge at a cost of $3800. Some of the remnants of this bridge can still be seen as you look downstream from the present steel-constructed bridge at the west end of town.

The Harrisburg Street Bridge as pictured was located at the north end of town. The previous bridge at this location was partially destroyed by the flood of 1889. Later, a center pier was placed under the bridge to strengthen the structure.

The covered bridge located at Brown's Dam (Hafers, Millers): This bridge, unlike most others, did not have the arch type of construction, but was carried by a truss work. The arch type was usually known as the Burr Truss, while other types were named after their original designers, such as: Town Truss, Howe Truss, McCullom Truss.

This bridge, known as the Peepytown Bridge, has been by-passed with a new bridge and highway. However, the covered bridge has been restored and is being preserved, for which we are most grateful.

Eisenhart's Bridge

There they are — those long, thin, steel rails stretching into infinity and leading you to the fondest dreams of traveling. If you look long and hard enough you can see and hear old number 6 heading directly toward you; and you question why the limping hobo doesn't move off the tracks. If you look closer, you may find that penny that was placed on the track for the engine to make you a "penny pancake." As you reach for the penny and your ear comes close to the ties, you can hear the musical rumbling of the steel wheels as they cross the links which connect the rails. Then, the low, shrill sound of a whistle echoes through the funnel of the trees letting you know that you will soon hear the creaking of the wooden ties as the massive weight of steel comes rolling over them.

In 1836, a meeting was held in East Berlin at the schoolhouse to consider the building of a railroad which would connect York and Gettysburg. An Act was passed to incorporate the Wrightsville and Gettysburg railroad. After the completion of this railroad, and the Hanover to Gettysburg link, a survey was made to extend a railroad line to East Berlin. J. S. Gitt, a civil engineer living in New Oxford made this survey in 1875-76 from Red Hill (5 miles west of Hanover) through Abbottstown and in to East Berlin.

A Charter was executed and the Berlin Branch Railroad Company was formed with A. W. Eichelberger of Hanover as president and A. U. Storm of East Berlin as Secretary-Treasurer. Shares, par value of fifty dollars, were sold to many residents of Abbottstown and East Berlin. East Berlin subscribed $27,000 and Abbottstown, $15,000. Later coupon bonds, face value of $100, were issued and sold to investors. The bond contained twenty coupons, valued at $3 each

No.

Shs.

Berlin Branch Rail Road Co.

OF PENNSYLVANIA.

SHARES $50,00 Each.

This is to Certify

Berlin, Pa.

Secretary. President.

and payable at the Hanover Saving Fund Society. The contractors were: Nicholas Fleigle, B. B. Gonder and Sons, Cyrus Diller and a few subscribers. L. Williams was the track layer. Construction was begun forthwith and the road was completed in 1877.

Preparing for the "Run"

Picking up the mail.

The freight is loaded.

Choosing the right track.

The billing is completed.

No. ______ East Berlin Station, Oct 17 1882

Mr. ______

To Hanover Junction, Hanover & Gettysburg R. R. Co., Dr.

For Freight from ______ per Manifest No. ______

on ______

MARKS.	WEIGHT.	RATE.	AMOUNT.
	80	8	.23
Expenses,			.23
			[illegible]

Received payment for the Company,

(Form [illegible]) ______ Agent.

The *branch train* ran seven miles to the "Y" or Junction to connect with the main line of the Western Maryland (one track). Once each morning, and again in the evening it made these scheduled runs starting from the "engine shed."

At one time, it was called the "Gospel Train," at other times it was called less religious names. The "Gospel" idea was born of the time when all three of its crewman — engineer, fireman, and conductor — were ministers of the Dunker Church. On one occasion, it began and completed its return trip from the Junction with the stranded conductor standing on the depot platform waving frantically; the *train* seemed to function just as well with a crew of two.

I'll see you back at the train, was a familiar call since many would be there to meet this interesting mode of transportation. It was something of a social gathering or rallying point for the youngsters as well as the adults.

As the *train* left East Berlin, it bore passengers for Gettysburg, Hanover or York. The back-road distance to York was twelve miles, while the distance by rail was thirty-two, giving some idea of its circuitous route. Returning, it brought the "Drummers" who would stay at the Shaffer House or the Sunday House while they worked the surrounding territory. As each "Drummer" stepped off the *train,* he was usually handed a card informing him that fine horses could be rented at the Livery Stable; you could see him heading west out of town early the next morning.

The touring businessman needs transportation.

The town businessman must travel.

The country doctor.

My Sunday afternoon rig.

A lady rides sidesaddle.

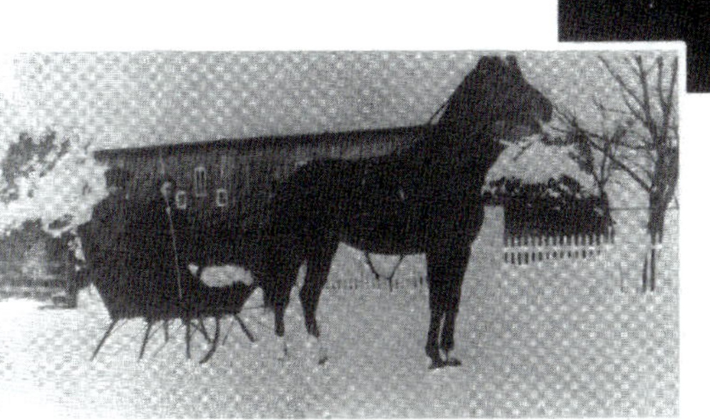

A winter sleigh ride.

The dusty street.

At the turn of the present century, the town had what was then called a "Stage Coach Line" running between East Berlin and York by the way of Abbottstown. It was a less expensive way of getting to York than via the runabout railroad route; hence, many people made use of the "Stage Coach." It wasn't long until the "Stage Coach line" began to lose revenue to that new innovation — the horseless carriage, or the *automobile*. As time progressed and *automobiles* became more numerous, the "Stage" became extinct.

For Pleasure

For Safety

Most of the early *automobiles* were used for both business and pleasure, as the one pictured here was used by the town doctor.

In 1920, after approximately a century of corporate and private ownership, the "Turnpike" from East Berlin to Hanover became a part of the State Highway System. With the improvement of automotive conveyance and roads, the *truck* became more useful and more important to the businesses of the town. The butcher, miller and others used the *truck* to make deliveries.

East Berlin's early *Bus* transportation: 1923-1947

The *railroad* operated under different management from time to time and was successful financially until the *automobile, truck* and *bus* began to attract passenger and freight business.

After the first decade of the twentieth century, the *railroad* was forced to curtail expenses; and the familiar whistle of *Locomotive No. 6* as it approached East Berlin no longer attracted the townspeople to the railroad station to see who was arriving or departing.

The "dinky" engine and the converted-gasoline-engine vehicle which did yeoman service hauling freight during the last years of the railroad no longer had any attraction for the curious observer. The death knell of the railroad had sounded!

On April 29, 1939 the shareholders of the Company voted to suspend operations pending permission being granted by the Pennsylvania Public Service Commission. The late William P. Baker was appointed *receiver* on April 13, 1942 for the purpose of completing distribution of the Company's assets. The rails were sold to a junk dealer, who was not slow in removing them from the roadbed. After all other property belonging to the Company had been disposed of, all indebtedness had been paid; the remaining money in the hands of the *receiver* was divided, pro rata, among all the shareholders who surrendered their stock certificates.

The evidence that East Berlin once had a *railroad* is fast disappearing. There still remains portions of the roadbed, mostly covered with brush where not farmed, approximately two hundred yards west and running parallel to the road from East Berlin to Abbottstown.

For the older people, the *railroad* is a happy memory; for the young, it will soon be a tradition.

1898

MAIN STREET
TRANSPORTATION
PROBLEMS

1960

Improved Main Street, 1963

BEAVER CREEK BRIDGE — EAST MAIN STREET

Yesteryear

Yesterday

Today

Harrisburg Street Bridge, 1964

West Main Street Bridge, 1964

RECREATION

RECREATION

Born of necessity from the neighboring woodlands and designed with a purpose in mind, I stand proudly as I stretch my arms from bank to bank. I was here before the town, and have watched it grow. Some times its growth was slow; and at times, its pace would quicken — but always it found room to spread and reach for greater things. Witnessing the sorrows and pleasures of the community leaves me with the knowledge that life is never simple.

My tasks have been numerous, and my burdens heavy. I have labored under the weight of Spring floods, and relaxed during the Summer drought. I have felt the tingle of falling leaves as they floated o'er me with the trickling water of the Fall showers. My still waters have felt the tinge of the wintry North wind, and have become frozen as far as my arms could reach. I have felt the warmth of the Spring sunshine and heard the cracking of the ice, only to know that my arms would creak from the strain of the thaw.

These old eyes have seen many things, both sad and pleasant. I have seen with joy the birth of a neighbor — the double covered bridge: only to shed tears when my eyes were covered with torrents of water and opened later to find my friend hurt and, then, removed. I have seen the sky aglow from the burning embers of my mill, and felt life anew to see it born again. I have seen the disappointment of the youth who lost his best fishing pole, only to find him back again trying to catch the big one. I have blushed to see young lovers stroll down the nearby lane, where they stopped and kissed. And, when those immodest swimmers come, I just close my eyes to preserve some dignity.

FISHIN
THE
AGELESS
SPORT

Boating

The old *Bass* fishing area.

Keeping cool in Summertime

Just one minute too late to see the "Skinny Dippers" in action.

The ice is fine.

Skating at the dam below the P.O.S. of A. Hall.

A sleigh ride through the beautiful, wintry countryside was always an enjoyable sport; a warm farm house with plenty of food was usually the termination point of sleighing parties.

Henry Sunday built a race track in 1905 behind the home now owned by Nevin Decker. However, not all of the town racing was held at this track. The creek, when frozen, made a wonderful track for the boys and young men to race their horses and sleighs. *They* usually had a good time, but annoyed the many skaters who also used the same area.

The Bicycle Club was formed in 1895. One of their longest trips was the one to Reading, Pennsylvania.

A hike to Pine Hill and the quarry to carve some initials on the rocks and trees.

Up in the Woods was the term used for the picnic grounds. The woods was owned by John Kuhn who cleared a large area and constructed a band stand, as well as, a dance floor. Here, an ice-cream cone could be purchased for a penny.

Sunday-afternoon water excursion

Chatter-Box Club: The needle experts

DO YOU REMEMBER:

Corner Ball: When the most important part of a public sale was the ball game in the barnyard that usually ended in a fight?

Box Socials: And the public programs by the pupils of the country schools, which were frequently held on Friday evenings?

Rattle Bands: The expected, unexpected, serenade of a newly married couple? (Length of serenade — until noisemakers were treated.)

Snitzing Party: Gathering apples to make apple-butter the next day?

Spelling Bee: A spelling contest for young and old at the local school?

Medicine Show: That wagon full of *free* entertainment that cost *so* much?

Pot Belly Stove: A round stove surrounded by benches in the country store, which were filled with male gossipers each evening?

Teen Center: Two decades ago

Corner Ball

BASEBALL

The country town was the seedbed of major league baseball players for many years. East Berlin was a *Baseball Town* shortly after the turn of the century — not that it had a good team every year, but it had its occasional *streaks* or *runs,* depending on the concentration of talent at a particular time. The years 1908 through 1911 marked a *heydey* of success.

Strangely, the game which put East Berlin's name on the front page of the sports' section of every Metropolitan newspaper on Sunday, August 6, 1911 was not a game which they won, but rather one which they lost. A twenty-inning game would have been newsworthy in the major leagues; but when two amateur teams go that far into extra innings, it merited the wires of the great news services. East Berlin lost this game to New Oxford, 5-4. Almost equally interesting, is the fact that it was the first game ever pitched by Don Mummert, and he went the full distance chalking up 24 strike-outs. Up to this time, he was a left-handed catcher; and baseball does not believe in left-handed catchers. Now, he would alternate his position.

The core of East Berlin's team was a high school team strengthened by some older players. It was an outstanding team of the area during its several peak years.

BOX SCORE

New Oxford	R	H	O	A	E	East Berlin	R	H	O	A	E
Roth, rf	1	0	5	0	0	Bally Lauber, ss	0	3	2	1	2
Smith, 3b	2	2	5	4	1	John Lauber, 3b	1	0	6	2	0
Miller, lf	0	1	6	1	0	Don Mummert, p	0	3	1	3	0
Brown, ss-p	1	2	3	8	0	Dut Resser, 1b	1	0	13	0	0
C. Hetzel, 2b	1	2	2	4	1	Chester Mummert, c	0	1	24	3	0
Dunn, 1b	0	2	26	1	2	Ed Emig, 2b	0	1	2	1	0
S. Kell, cf	0	1	6	2	1	Herb Eisenhart, lf	1	2	8	1	0
Sadler, c	0	3	6	2	0	Elmer Gruver, rf	1	1	1	0	1
Beavenour, p-ss	0	1	1	4	0	Bob Weaver, cf	0	1	3	1	1
	5	14	60	26	5		4	12	60	12	4

New Oxford: 1 1 0 0 0 1 0 0 1 0 0 0 0 0 0 0 0 0 0 1 — 5
East Berlin: 1 0 2 0 0 0 0 0 1 0 0 0 0 0 0 0 0 0 0 0 — 4

As in every good story, there is always a happy ending; East Berlin defeated New Oxford in the next two games of the series, 2-1 and 9-4.

Cheerleaders for a great team

Early High School Team

Constitution

Section 1

Art 1 The name and Style of this Society shall be the "[illegible] Improvement Society."

Art 2 The object of this Society shall be to promote the improvement of its Members in reading and Criticism.

Art 3 No person shall be admitted a Member of this Society but by a vote of two thirds of the Members present.

Art 4 This Society shall meet as often as may be deemed expedient, and five members shall constitute a Quorum.

Art 5 The Officers of this Society shall be a President, Vice President, and Secretary and Treasurer in one, who shall be elected Quarterly, and if the election take place at the end of the term for which they were elected they [illegible] continue in Office until others be elected.

Art 11 Any Member guilty of ungentlemanly Conduct, shall be expelled, but none shall be expelled but by a vote of two thirds of the Members present, and if any Member leave the room without leave of the President during the transaction of business, shall pay a fine of five cents for the first offence, ten for the second, and for the third offence to be expelled from the Society.

Sec. 5. Of the Powers of the Society.

Art 12 The Society shall have power to adopt By Laws for the transaction of business, if not inconsistent with this Constitution, and all the Amendments to the Constitution shall be proposed in writing, and if approved by two thirds of the Members present, shall be annexed to the foregoing Articles.

Saturday Evening [illegible]

The meeting being called to order the minutes of the preceding meeting were then read.

R. N. Hutchison from the committee on damages reports the books returned all in good order.

The Secretary laid before the Society A Bill to establish a presentation from the Hon. Moses McClean, viz, A Bill to establish a Smithsonian Institution at Washington for the Diffusion of Knowledge at Washington City. [illegible] this association [illegible] a thanks of [illegible] Absentees [illegible] Hildebrand, S. I. Wolf, [illegible] Miller, [illegible] Hildebrand, and [illegible] Miller. No other business being before the House the Society adjourned until

valuable donations

C. [illegible] Hildebrand Chairman of the com. on the library laid before the society the presentation of [illegible] from the Hon. Moses McClean.

Letters were then read from the following persons who were elected honorary Members of this association viz.

Daniel Eastman	York Springs
James Buchanan	Washington
Wm. P. Maulsby	Westminster
A. G. Eye	Annapolis
& James X. McLanahan	Chambersburg

Mr. McLanahan recommending to the Society in his letter the adoption of a Motto, the language of the Father of his Country viz.

"In proportion as the structure of Government gives force to Public Opinion it is essential that

R. [illegible] Heitzell, from the com. on damages reports the books all in good order.

I. [illegible] from the committee to revise the constitution reports that they have performed their duty. The constitution as revised was adopted.

The resolution to amend the 7th art of the constitution was [illegible].

The following resolution was offered & laid on the table,

Resolved, That the 9th art of the Constitution be amended, as to read thus; Every member refusing to read, when called upon by the President, shall pay a fine of six & a fourth cents. Providing: that this be of no effect on female members

EAST BERLIN COMMUNITY PARK

In late 2004, the East Berlin Borough Council created a Parks & Recreation Commission. Its purpose was to develop a borough owned tract of 17-acres as a park & recreation area on North Avenue.

In 2011, Phase I of the park was completed with primary features being a 1,250 square-foot picnic pavilion, a skate park, a 0.4-mile walking path, a personalized brick walkway, and a paved entrance and parking area. The park receives daily use and special community events are held throughout the year.

To continue to develop the park with features such as a playground, soccer fields, basketball and tennis courts, etc, financial support will be an ongoing need. Donations can be directed to the Borough Office. Other options of providing financial support can be made by supporting our "Engrave a Brick" program or sponsorship of a picnic table. The "Engrave a Brick" program has been popular as one can use it to honor, memorialize, or acknowledge people, pets, or achievements. The brick is placed in the brick walkway, and its individual personalized bricks have become a good conversation starter for park visitors. Sponsoring of picnic tables produces the same response from visitors as a plaque is attached to the picnic table with wording of the sponsor's choice. The picnic pavilion, with a capacity of at least 80, can also be reserved for exclusive use at a daily fee of $50. Proceeds from the pavilion rental help park funding, as well.

SERVICE

SERVICE

ALUMNI ASSOCIATION — EAST BERLIN HIGH SCHOOL

Through the interest of members of the Class of 1936 of the East Berlin High School, and with the cooperation of Principal E. M. Gruver, efforts were made to form an Alumni Association.

After several preliminary meetings, an organizational meeting was held in the school building on September 2, 1936 at which time committees were named and the following officers elected: *President,* John H. Myers, '22; *Vice-President,* Charles Gentzler, '19; *Secretary,* Mary Ida Mummert Brown, '34; *Assistant Secretary,* Ethel Resser, '18; *Treasurer,* Glenn Boyer, '31.

On September 30, 1936, a proposed constitution was unanimously adopted and a resolution passed to award a medal to the *first* honor student of each graduating class.

A special meeting was held on December 30, 1936 to plan for the first annual banquet which was held at the West York Inn on March 27, 1937 with 69 in attendance. Banquet attendance ranged from a low of 41 in 1945 to the high in 1962 and 1963 when reservations were closed at 250 and 370, respectively. Reunion classes made special efforts to be well represented.

The first mailing list to be completed in full, with the exception of 5 alumni, was compiled in the latter half of 1961 by E. M. Gruver. The listing included names and addresses of alumni beginning with the Class of 1909, when the high school was first recognized by the State Department, through 1957, when a change was made by Jointure Consolidation. Fewer than three percent of the alumni are deceased.

Receipts from plays presented annually from 1936 to 1941 by members of the Association were used to purchase a three-program electric clock, lengthen stage curtain valance, provide annual scholarship medals and offer $125 toward concreting locker-room floors. A $100 bond, purchased in 1942, remains in a savings account.

Present officers are: *President,* E. M. Gruver, '12; *Vice President,* Carlton Jacobs, '39; *Secretary,* Ruth Ziegler Frey, '43; *Assistant Secretary,* Phyllis Glatfelter Trimmer, '50; *Treasurer,* Robert Trimmer, '50; *Assistant Treasurer,* John Wisler, '38.

BOY SCOUTS

The Boy-Scout program was introduced to East Berlin in 1912 as Troop 111 and is still registered under the same number at the present time.

Few records are available of the Troop at the time of its organization. It is said, however, that fourteen boys joined the troop; they went camping at Brown's Dam.

Little is known of the Troop until 1919 when Reverend Harry Kehm was Scoutmaster. At this time, the Troop had eighteen members.

Richard Reynolds took over the Troop in 1920; and from this time until 1932, few records exist. The Troop disbanded and reorganized several times during its early years.

Reorganization took place in 1932 when a group of citizens recruited William Sinner to be Scoutmaster and Doctor Eugene Elgin as Chairman. The Reverend Houtz replaced Doctor Elgin as Chairman in 1933. The Troop remained the same until 1936 with the average registration of thirteen to sixteen boys.

Oniska Tribe #40, I.O.R.M. took over as sponsor of the Troop in 1936 with Sheldon Mosler as Scoutmaster and twelve boys registered.

The next sponsor was the East Berlin Lions Club in 1940. Richard Eustice was Scoutmaster and Richard Riggs the Chairman.

A group of citizens became sponsors of the Troop in 1943. Leonard Myers was Scoutmaster and Charles Gentzler the Chairman.

The Troop disbanded in 1945 and in 1947 reorganization took place with Calvin Lerew as Scoutmaster and C. D. Krout the Chairman. At the end of this year the Troop was again disbanded.

In November, 1957 the Troop was reorganized and sponsored by the V.F.W. Richard Wise was Scoutmaster and Irwin Gross the Chairman. The Troop remained the same for three years when Charles Fetrow became Scoutmaster and Leonard Myers the Chairman.

Some of the highlights from 1957 to the present time were the following: Troop 111 had forty-four boys participating in the last Haines' Safari, Haines Acres, York, Pennsylvania. Of the participating troops, East Berlin's was one of the largest.

Two boys have taken the Canadian Canoe Trip; this trip is sponsored by the York-Adams Area Council, Boy Scouts of America. On this trip, the boys are taken through the Canadian wilds.

The Council sponsored the trip to Norfolk, Virginia. Troop 111 had two boys participating in this trip.

Troop 111's first Eagle Scout was Thomas O. Myers; he was the recipient of this award in 1962. In November, 1963 we had two more boys reach the rank of Eagle Scouts; they were James Menges and Ronald Chronister.

GIRL SCOUTS

We hold that ultimate responsibility for the Girl Scout movement rests with Volunteers. This quote is taken from the preamble of the Constitution of Girl Scouts of the United States of America. In the organizational year of 1944, Kathryn Miller was the leader with the following people serving as committee members: Mrs. Robert Lau, Mrs. Mildred Eck, Mrs. Ethel Altland, Mrs. Hazel Hoffman, and Mrs. Richard Shaffer.

Troop #1 included these girls: Peggy Moul, Doris Pifer, Mary Eisenhart, Martha Eisenhart, Dottie Mae Resser, Miriam Klinedinst, Doris Myers, Margaret Leas, Gloria Spangler, Marilyn Hoover, and Geraldine Lemmon.

Over the years, various troops and numbers have been assigned to the following leaders: Intermediate Troop #1 — Miss Kathryn Miller, Mrs. Robert Lau; Troop #5 — Julia Glatfelter, Mrs. Beatrice Debolt, Mrs. Florence Hull, Mrs. Ellen Hinkle, and Lois Baker; Senior Troop #40 — Mrs. Mary Ida Brown; Senior Troop #69 — Mrs. Pauline Baum and Mrs. Ellen Hinkle; Brownie Troop #38 — Mrs. Bruce McClay, Mrs. Doris Leister, Mrs. Harriet Myers, Mrs. Lois Eisenhart, Mrs. Adath Cramer, and Mrs. Elaine Lerew.

The Troops listed their activties proudly over the years; some of these were: Christmas caroling, merit-badge work, money for needy families and Red Cross, favors for shut-ins, hikes, camp-outs and hayrides. In addition, some of the major events in which the East Berlin Troops have participated include: Scout Jamborees, the Juliette Lowe Rallies. The money for these worthy affairs was raised by collecting fat, scrap and by selling cookies.

In 1947, the East Berlin girls reached the rank of first-class Scouts and in 1955 helped in the purchase of Camp Happy Valley by selling 85 dozen boxes of cookies (the most sold by a troop in Adams County). Trees were planted in honor of the girls at the new camp site.

One brave secretary wrote in the minutes, *Some of us worked on badges and some carried on.* In any event, many accomplishments were realized with the most recent one being Bonnie Lusk's winning the highest award in Scouting; she received the curved bar in 1961.

Commendable, isn't it? And to think that all this is done by volunteers!

The current leaders are: Mrs. Janet Howe, Mrs. Elaine Lerew, Mrs. Lois Baker, and Mrs. Ellen Hinkle.

LIBERTY FIRE COMPANY — LADIES' AUXILIARY

Pursuant to requests from members of the Company for a Ladies' Auxiliary, interested ladies were invited to attend a meeting. Fourteen ladies braved the cold, snowy night on January 4, 1941 resulting in the temporary president, Mrs. Rosella Altland, requesting another meeting with more interested ladies present.

Archie Himes on January 27, 1941 conducted the election of officers for the new group as follows: *President,* Rosella Altland; *Vice-President,* Elizabeth Mummert; *Secretary,* Dolly McIntire; *Treasurer,* Frances Jacobs.

The original meeting night — the first Monday of the month — has not been changed through the years; the dues have been increased several times from the initial five cents per month to the present two dollars per year.

The Constitution and By-Laws were adopted on March 3, 1941. Katie Slothour was appointed to the newly created post of Chaplain in 1944.

The Ladies' Auxiliary of the Fire Company has served the Company and community well as is evidenced by the many activities listed here: aided the Company in the purchase of capes and caps, aided in War-Bond drives; sponsored Girl-Scout Troops; furnished raincoats for School Safety Patrols; conducts annual Easter-Egg hunt; assists at the annual carnival and contributes cash donations to the Fire Company.

The present officers are: Lois Eisenhart, *President*; Alice Altland, *Vice-President;* Joyce Shafer, *Secretary;* Mary Markley, *Treasurer*; Grace Stambaugh, *Chaplain;* Barbara Shafer, *Corresponding Secretary.* The current membership is 98.

HIGH SCHOOL WAR EFFORT

Starting in the latter part of June, 1942, about fifty students harvested 17,653 pounds of cherries for the Nunda Fruit Farm in less than two days. This same force moved into the Spencer Snyder orchards the following morning where in eight days, more than 60,000 pounds of cherries were checked in. During this same time, another group of approximately the same number of students took over the harvesting of the A. B. C. Williams' crop. Here, in two weeks, about 80,000 pounds were harvested. This would indicate that altogether these students picked more than 157,000 pounds of cherries, most of which were packed for the armed forces. During the latter part of the summer, these same groups harvested beans, tomatoes, peaches, and early varieties of apples.

School opened on Tuesday, September 8; and after nine days of school, the high school was closed for two weeks to permit students to assist with apple picking and general farm work. This shutdown was followed by six half-day sessions starting at 8:00 a.m. and closing at 11:00 a.m. Students assisting in orchards came clothed for work and carried their lunches. By this plan it was possible to have the pickers in the orchards by noon. More than 25,000 bushels were picked at the Nunda orchards, while more than 45,000 bushels were harvested from the H. M. Weigle orchards near Idaville.

According to reports, East Berlin High School had the only completely school-organized, school-supervised, student-workers' program in the State. Since about forty per cent of the pickers were girls and many of the boys too small to handle long ladders, some of which were twenty-four feet in length, ladder setters were employed. This arrangement made possible the harvesting of much fruit which otherwise would have spoiled and also provided necessary protection for the trees.

The best day's pick for a boy was 176 bushels, while 81 was the high for a girl. One boy's season record was 2,067 bushels, as compared with 1,337 for a girl. A grand total of more than $9000 was earned by these students. Much of the earned money was used to purchase War Bonds and, in many cases, used to finance further education.

IMPROVED ORDER OF RED MEN — ONISKA TRIBE #40

The IMPROVED ORDER OF RED MEN is the lineal descendant of the SONS OF LIBERTY, who for more than ten years prior to the Declaration of Independence, had by their active work paved the way for that immortal act. When the SONS OF LIBERTY in many localities merged into Societies of St. Tamina, from 1771 to 1800, the love of country and the conservation of liberty were still the guiding impulse. In 1813 it took on another form in the Society of Red Men, formed at Fort Mifflin. Under this name it existed for nearly twenty years. From 1828 to 1832, the Society of Red Men languished and became nearly extinct. In 1833, interest was revitalized. By adding to its patriotic and fraternal features the charitable and benevolent work of its present ministrations, the Improved Order of Red Men was initiated.

Thus has come to us the glorious trinity of our inspiring motto — *FREEDOM, FRIENDSHIP* and *CHARITY* — and by it is recorded the origin and growth of our affiliation. The Sons of Liberty gave us *Freedom;* the Tammany Societies and the Society of Red Men added *Friendship.* The Improved Order of Red Men consecrated the work of *Charity.*

A petition for the organization of a Great Council in Pennsylvania, dated February 25, 1849, was signed by the first five Tribes organized in Pennsylvania. It was granted, and the first Council Brand of the Great Council of Pennsylvania was lit May 23, 1849 in Philadelphia. The 40th tribe to be instituted in this great reservation was Oniska Tribe No. 40 on April 23, 1857. Of the 39 Tribes instituted prior to No. 40, there are three in existence today.

The first meeting for the institution of Oniska Tribe was held in the Church School House on February 21, 1857. William Wolf was appointed president and George W. Hildebrand, secretary. A committee was appointed to petition the Great Council of Pennsylvania for a charter.

At the meeting of March 28, 1857, the following members were elected as officers: *Sacham,* George Schwartz, *Senior Sagamore,* F. B. Raber; *Junior Sagamore,* G. H. Shaffer; *Chief of Records,* B. Hildebrand; *Keeper of Wampum,* William Wolf; *Prophet,* Francis Hildebrand; *Trustees,* Misenhelder, Wolf, and George Shaffer.

The tribe held together until about 1870 when some of the members became dissatisfied and stampeded the tribe with their wampum belt and joined an organization in East Berlin known as the "True Blues."

In 1871, four members of the old organization and eleven new members relit the council fire; the old members which were responsible for the relighting of the council fire were: H. W. King, George Baucher, John Giselman and I. S. Trostle. The Pale Faces were J. Curtis Hildebrand, Michael McSherry, D. S. Bender, F. C. Wolf, J. Henry Bahn, Israel Stambaugh, John Getz, John Weist, A. S. Trostle, C. W. Baker and John Miller. The council fire was again lit in the old Church School, and they later moved to the hall which they purchased in 1888.

In 1914, one of the members of Oniska started out to organize a tribe in the hunting grounds of York Springs; and on the 21st day of April, 1914 his ambition was realized and the council fire of Metossa Tribe of York Springs No. 263 was lit with a membership of 45. It later grew to a membership of 86. However, in 1933 this tribe cried out in distress; on March 27, 1933, it was consolidated with Oniska Tribe with 13 members. Oniska was always a small tribe; fifty years ago the membership numbered 40. Today, while nearly all organizations of this type have disbanded, No. 40 has 100 members in good standing. The highest number of members in the organization's history was 125.

Back in the early 1900's, the Improved Order of Red Men instituted a plan paying benefits to orphans of the Order. This was a grand plan at a time when there was no welfare organization as there is today. Oniska paid relief to the Harry Resser orphans, the Ursinus Glatfelter orphans and the Chester Hull orphans. In recent years, welfare organizations have assumed the responsibility of this type of work; but the I.O.R.M. still has a responsibility to the welfare of its orphans.

After 108 years, Oniska Tribe looks with pride at its record of paying thousands of dollars in sick-and-death benefits. The organization is still in healthy condition and holds meetings every Monday evening in their Wigwam on West King Street.

The first 15 feet of the main building of the meeting hall was built prior to the year 1849 and the balance of the main building was built shortly thereafter. The main hall was first built for a carriage shop on the lower floor; and the second floor was used for small traveling shows, which were quite numerous in the early days.

VETERANS OF FOREIGN WARS

The pre-organizational work of the Richard J. Gross Post, No. 8896, began in the latter part of 1946. The purposes of the V.F.W. are recognized for their *Fraternal, Patriotic, Historical, and Educational* betterment programs.

Robert S. Musser, the man considered to be the *father* of the Post, along with David Krout, a former member of White Rose Post, No. 556, started contacting men in World Wars I and II to interest them in organizing a Veterans of Foreign Wars Post in East Berlin. Interest mounted in this worthy endeavor since the returning veterans were eager to be a part of a unified organization.

The first official meeting was held February 13, 1947 with Robert S. Musser in command. At this organizational session, the following staff of officers was elected: *Commander*, David Krout; *Senior Vice-Commander*, Raymond Hoffman, Sr.; *Junior Vice-Commander*, Edgar Baker; *Quartermaster*, Irwin Gross; *Adjutant*, Paul Fahs; *Officer of the Day*, Clarence Horn; *Chaplain*, Victor Glatfelter. At this meeting, the Town Council gave its permission for the organization to hold the meeting in the Fire Hall.

The Charter was signed and sent to the Department of Pennsylvania, VFW, and approved March 13, 1947. The name given to the Post was Richard J. Gross Post 8896. This name was selected in honor of Richard J. Gross, the first man from the community of East Berlin to lose his life in World War II. As an Army Air Force soldier he was killed in a crash of a B-24 over New Guinea on September 8, 1943.

One of the first official acts was to appoint a building committee to secure a site for a post home. After the site was secured on September 11, 1947 a building committee was appointed as follows: Gene Tanner; Clarence Horn, Sr.; Kenneth Darone, John Wisler and George Berkheimer. Soon after the building committee began to function, the Home Association was formed; and an application was made to transfer the property from the Post to the Home Association. During the building of the Home, many members put all their spare time in helping with the work; and on October 9, 1947, they held their meeting in the "shell" of the building.

A great milestone in the growth and development of the Home came four years later when the mortgage on the building was burned.

Included among the achievements of the Post are: the organization and support of a ball team, a dart team and a rifle club; the organization of the firing squad and purchasing uniforms for this group; the sponsoring of annual parties at Halloween and Christmas for members' children.

One of the outstanding highlights of the Post's history concerns the event on February, 1953 when the Post was host to the Honorable George F. Kennan, former Ambassador to Russia. A return visit was made the following year by Mr. Kennan at which time he was presented a citation from the Post. Scenes of the presentation were televised giving the Post recognition throughout the State.

The Post was honored with the twenty-first District encampment. Post Commander Allen Moul was elected Commander of the District and given a life membership to the National Organization.

Fund-raising projects were started in conjunction with the Home Association, due to the plan to erect a new Home. On October 27, 1956 ground-breaking ceremonies were held. The new Post Home shares with the community its spacious auditorium showing unity of spirit.

The current membership is 283.

LIONS CLUB

The East Berlin Lions Club was organized on May 19, 1939 with E. G. Moyer, International Counselor presiding.

The first known officers were: *President*, J. E. Gentzler; *1st Vice-President,* the Reverend Richard Shaffer; *2nd Vice-President*, Paul P. Lerew; *3rd Vice-President*, Elmer M. Gruver; *Secretary*, C. D. Krout.

There were twenty-five charter members as follows: V. Y. Brandt, John Berkheimer, John W. Bankert, N. G. Decker, Richard G. Eustice, Harry Emig, J. E. Gentzler, Purley Grove, George R. Glatfelter, E. M. Gruver, Dr. Allen W. Kelly, David S. Kime, C. D. Krout, Paul P. Lerew, W. Denton Myers, George W. Moul, John Myers, George E. Mummert, Dr. Roy E. Smith, the Reverend Richard Shaffer, the Reverend John R. Strevig, L. D. Spangler, George L. Shetter, L. L. Smith, M. Edwin Webb.

In 1953, the Club became known as the Beaver Creek Lions Club with Amos H. Kuhn as President and George G. Hollinger, Jr. as Secretary; and in 1957 the Club joined with the Abbottstown Club.

A new East Berlin Lions Club, sponsored by the Beaver Creek Lions Club, was organized on August 27, 1957 in Zwingli Reformed Church through the assistance of State Secretary-Treasurer, Junius M. Chestnutt; District Governor, Sidney Bernsteen; International Counsellors, James E. Gilman and Carroll E. Dull; Deputy District Governor, William E. Lau and Beaver Creek President, Earl E. Alwine.

The following were elected to serve as the officers of the new club: *President,* Ralph Eisenhart; *1st Vice-President*, Charles B. Wallace; *2nd Vice-President*, Glenn Cashman; *3rd Vice-President*, Luther Smith; *Secretary*, Robert Potts; *Treasurer,* Ralph Boyer; *Lion Tamer*, Charles Spangler; *Tail Twister*, William Martin; *Directors,* Leon Roos, 1957 to 1959; Wilson Streightiff, 1957 to 1959; C. Richard Emig, 1957 to 1958; Raymond Jacobs, 1957 to 1958.

The charter members of the new East Berlin Club are: Ralph Boyer, Glenn Cashman, C. Richard Emig, James R. Eisenhart, Ralph Eisenhart, John Gruver, Raymond Jacobs, Mervin R. Lau, Donald R. Moul, John Philips, Dr. Robert Potts, Richard O. Riggs, Paul J. Lerew, Lynn D. Slothour, Joel N. Tanner, Charles B. Wallace, Sherman B. Krall, John G. Leib, Allen W. Moul, Luther P. Smith, Charles L. Spangler, Glenn C. Herman, Dr. Leon Roos, Wilson Streightiff, William Martin.

Charter night was observed by the Club on December 12, 1957. President Ralph E. Eisenhart received the charter dated December 5, 1957.

The purpose of the Lions Club is spelled out in their slogan . . . *L — Liberty; I — Intelligence; O — Our; N — Nation's; S — Safety.*

In fulfilling the purposes, the Club has conducted many worthy projects for the benefit of the community. We list some of them here: purchased ambulance stretcher, eye glasses, merit-badge scouting books, and street-name signs for East Berlin and Hampton; provided portable public-address system for community use and waste receptacles for the Borough streets; sponsored learn-to-swim program with more than 150 children participating each year, the Girl Scout Troop, and the dedication program of the Borough's new post-office building; co-sponsored the athletic night honoring the athletes in the Bermudian Springs High School; the Club contributes financial support to Beacon Lodge (a recreation camp for the blind), and to the Northeast Pennsylvania Lions Eye Bank; distributes welfare gifts and Christmas baskets and decorates the Borough streets at Christmas season; placed picnic tables in two different areas for use by the public.

Our motto "We Serve" can be displayed proudly by all members.

The officers of the East Berlin Club for 1963-64 are: *President,* Paul J. Lerew; *1st Vice-President,* the Reverend William Anderman, Jr.; *2nd Vice-President,* Wayne Lau; *3rd Vice-President,* Alfred R. Billett; *Secretary,* G. Frederick Howe; *Treasurer,* Harry R. Albert; *Tail Twister,* Stephen Heyser; *Lion Tamer,* Paul H. Wolf; *Directors,* Charles Fahs, Mervin E. Chronister, Chester Hoff, C. Richard Emig.

LIONS CHARTER NIGHT

The Club, in its most recent service to the community, contacted organizations and businesses for financial assistance and volunteer help in the restoration of the Church School House. The building, located on the East Berlin Union Cemetery bordering North Avenue, was used by early residents for meetings of the Berlin Improvement Society, Borough Council, voting polls, church and Sunday school, and public school.

Since the building was used recently for cemetery-equipment storage, the Club is spearheading a movement to build a new storage building so the Church School House can be restored as nearly like the original setting as possible.

PARENT-TEACHER ASSOCIATION

A group of interested parents and teachers of the East Berlin School met on September 13, 1948 in the auditorium of the school to organize a Parent-Teacher Association. After some discussion on the objectives and purposes of the organization, the following officers were elected: *President,* Eugene Tanner; *Vice-President,* Mrs. Mervin Jacobs; *Secretary,* Mrs. Elmer Mummert; *Treasurer,* Joseph Stoner. Conewago Jointure P.T.A. was selected as the name of the organization since membership was open to all who resided with the jointure. It was decided that the organization should become affiliated with both State and National Parent-Teacher Associations.

Several projects of the organization included the purchase of raincoats for the School Safety Patrol and raising of funds for the purchase of playground equipment.

From May 1955 until September 1960, the organization was inactive. However, during this period, an active organization continued to function in Reading Township. Since additional facilities became available in East Berlin, all one-room schools in Reading Township were closed and the children transported to East Berlin. At this time, steps were taken to organize a P.T.A. unit in cooperation with the Reading Township Association. This new organization was named the East Berlin P.T.A. Unit of the Bermudian Springs Joint School System.

Although this Association has been in operation for a very few years, additional playground equipment has been provided; and many volumes have been added to the centralized library. However, the chief accomplishment has been the cultivation of better understanding between the home and the school.

IMPROVED ORDER OF RED MEN SAGO COUNCIL 140 — DEGREE OF POCAHONTAS

On the thirtieth Sun of Worm Moon, G.S.D. 436, (March 30, 1927), Oniska Council 292, with a membership of 37, was instituted in East Berlin with Katie Slothour as *Prophetess*; Alverta Shetter, *Pocahontas*; Mary Lapham, *Wenonah*; George Hull, *Powhatan*; Ruth Butt, *Keeper of Records*; Estella Hamme, *Collector of Wampum* and Ethel Philips, *Keeper of Wampum*; dissolved on the Seventeenth Sun, Sturgeon Moon, G.S.D. 436, (August 17, 1927), and reorganized with 26 members as Sago Council 140, on the Fourteenth Sun, Traveling Moon, G.S.D. 470, (October 14, 1961), with Rosella Altland as *Prophetess*; Joyce Philips, *Pocahontas*; Peggy Willet, *Wenonah*; H. John Philips, *Powhatan*; Helen Altland, *Keeper of Records*; Beverly Glatfelter, *Collector of Wampum*; and Sylvia Herman, *Keeper of Wampum*.

Sago Council 140 now has a membership of 30 and meets in the Wigwam of Oniska Tribe 40, Improved Order of Red Men, the second and fourth Tuesday of each moon.

In 1883, Pocahontas Council No. 1 of Marblehead, Massachusetts, started the organization which has since crystalized in to the Degree of Pocahontas thus providing a living monument to Her Majesty, Queen Pocahontas.

The monument to Pocahontas will live so long as women and men join the Degree of Pocahontas and practice the virtues of this heroine of Virginia who so nobly exemplified our precepts, *Freedom — Friendship — Charity*. May we the members of this truly American Fraternity so exemplify, in our dealings with our Sisters and Brothers, the virtues of this beautiful American Heroine, that we may hand to posterity this living monument to Queen Pocahontas untarnished and may posterity be proud to carry this monument to generations unborn.

LIBERTY FIRE COMPANY

The first historical data to be located concerning the Liberty Fire Company, No. 1, of East Berlin, was the dedication of the Engine House on Saturday, October 22, 1892.

The first minutes, dated December 2, 1896, show a record of a reorganization meeting of the Liberty Fire Company of East Berlin, Pennsylvania.

The officers who served were: *President*, F. R. Darone; *Secretary*, C. Harry Myers; *Chief and Treasurer*, W. C. Leib.

The company purchased a carriage at Carlisle on August 9, 1898 for $400.

Uniforms were purchased for the company on August 14, 1900. Twenty-five uniforms were ordered at $9 each.

On August 26, 1921 fifty-six uniforms were purchased from the George Evans Company, Philadelphia, at $16.35 each.

Liberty Fire Company, East Berlin, was incorporated November 19, 1924.

A Lafrance 300-gallon pumper mounted on a Brochway chassis equipped with a 30-gallon soda-acid extinguisher and other accessories were purchased for $5500.

AMBASSADOR
GEORGE KENNAN

LIBERTY FIRE CO. No.1

Through the years, many important events have been recorded in the minute book of the Liberty Fire Company, including: February 9, 1937 — sent to Gettysburg $239.05 plus a truckload of food and clothing for the Ohio and Mississippi Flood Valley disaster victims; September, 1946 — a Dodge chassis equipped with American Marsh fire fighting equipment was purchased for $6300, equipment included a 500-gallon pumper, portable pump and a 350-gallon booster tank; 1953 — purchased the present Fire Hall from David S. Kime for $30,000; 1954 — Lerew's, Incorporated, donated a 1942 chassis (Ford) to the Fire Company, the members coverted same into a 1000-gallon tank truck; 1958 — an addition for housing equipment was added to the Fire House in 1958 at a cost of $12,000, moved equipment from Borough Hall to Company's building, building was dedicated during this year; a siren was purchased; *Sparky*, the company's mascot, was purchased in 1959; 1961 — a 1961 Ford, F1100 equipped with American LaFrance equipment was purchased for $28,600. The new equipment included: a 1000-gallon mid-ship pump, a high-pressure fog, 7-man cab, a portable light plant, a portable pump and other accessories.

The fire-police group was organized by the Company in 1963; the captain is John Kohler.

Present officers of the Company are: *President*, Earl Bollinger; *Secretary*, A. D. Himes, *Treasurer*, Melvin Rohrbaugh; *Chief*, Melvin Eisenhart; *Assistant Chief*, Kurvin Krout.

An ambulance Club was sponsored in 1958 by the Fire Company, and a 1956 Cadillac ambulance was purchased for $5400. This ambulance was replaced with a 1961 model in February 1964. Present officers of the Ambulance Club are: *President*, John Kohler; *Secretary*, Carlton Jacobs; *Treasurer*, Paul Corwin.

VETERANS OF FOREIGN WARS — LADIES' AUXILIARY

The Ladies' Auxiliary of Post No. 8896 was instituted at a meeting held in the Richard J. Gross Post on March 9, 1949. Ellen Swartz, then 21st District President, assisted by Mrs. Thea McCloskey and Mrs. Eva Boose, instituted the organization according to the National By-Laws. Elaine Lerew was elected to serve as the first president. The following charter members were initiated into the Auxiliary: Rosella Altland, Treva Chronister, Beatrice Debolt, Carrie Eisenhart, Louise Eisenhart, Margaret Eisenhart, Millie Eisenhart, Dorothy Gentzler, Lola Gross, Helena Gulden, Madaline Heberlien, Bernice Hoffman, Ethel Krout, Annie Leas, Ada Lehr, Elaine Lerew, Luella Lerew, Loretta Lucabaugh, Dolly Menges, Ruth Moul, Anna Perry, Florence Rohrbaugh, Melissa Roos, Erma Smyers, Agnes Spangler, Neva Spangler, Ruthetta Stambaugh, Jean Wisler, Maryann Ziegler. The Auxiliary now numbers 70.

The Auxiliary has been active in many pursuits through the years and are continuing to perform meritoriously in the following manner: assists the Post with the community Halloween and Christmas parties, with the summer picnic for the children at the Scotland Orphan's School and with services memorializing the war dead. In addition, the Auxiliary has held a Variety Show annually for the benefit of the fund for hospital work. It visits the Samuel G. Dixon Hospital at Mt. Alto and the Lebanon and Coatesville VA Hospitals giving stamps, clothing, stationery and toilet articles to those confined at these hospitals. Many accomplishments were concerned with the Post Home, including: providing drapes and venetian blinds, cabinets for the kitchen and the purchase of a coffee urn.

In September, 1952 the Auxiliary paid respects to the following Gold Star Mothers by making them honorary members: Emma Oberlander, Nettie Bollinger, Bertha Baker, and Sarah Gross.

The Auxiliary has made every effort to promote and aid in all civic affairs. At the State Convention held in Pittsburgh in July, 1961 the Post and Auxiliary received a National Citation for service to the community. The award was based on 5,163 hours and $2,163 contributed by Auxiliary and Post members in Community Service work — more than 1000 hours contributed in scout work alone.

The Auxiliary has attempted to keep the goal uppermost in thought and action:

To honor the dead by remembering the living.

RICHARD J. GROSS POST 8896 -VETERANS OF FOREIGN WARS

Richard J. Gross was born February 17, 1919, in York County. He graduated from East Berlin High School in May 1938. After his graduation, he was employed in the Hanover area and later at the Middletown Air Force Base. At the start of World War II, he tried to enlist in the service twice before he was finally accepted. He was inducted in the Army Air Force in June of 1942, at the New Cumberland Induction Center. He was sent to Kessler Field, Mississippi for basic training, then to Sioux Falls Radio School and from there to Gunnery School at Harlington, Texas. He left the United States from San Francisco and was sent to Port Moresby in New Guinea. Richard Gross' plane went down while flying a combat mission over New Guinea. He was acting as the radio operator-gunner on a B-24 Liberator Bomber when his plane went down. None of the crew survived. On September 8, 1943, he paid the Supreme Sacrifice for his country. The Richard J. Gross VFW Post was named in his honor.

Since 1956, the Post Home has made many additions and changes and is currently an integral part of the East Berlin community.

The new Post Home is a two-story cinder block building. The original first floor consisted of the kitchen, canteen, small game room, storage vault and restrooms. The second floor was built to serve as an auditorium and meeting room. The hall has been host to many community and Post activities over the years; such as dances, community activities for the youth, bingo, meetings and banquets. The new Post Home was dedicated on June 22, 1957.

In 1982 through 1983, a large renovation was made to the original Post Home. A wall was knocked out in order to enlarge the canteen, and the building was extended up two stories. A new bar was installed, and the kitchen was renovated.

The last change made to the Post Home was started in June 1998 and completed in February 1999. Those renovations included an up-to-date kitchen, remodeled existing restrooms and added additional rest rooms upstairs, an office/conference room was added upstairs, and a handicapped elevator was installed.

In the early 1960's, a Memorial Stone was placed in front of the Post Home in remembrance of departed comrades. In 1990, the Ladies Auxiliary requested a similar memorial stone for their departed sisters. The VFW Board agreed to add "and sister" to their stone. In September 1970, two 16-inch battleship shells were placed on each side of the memorial stone; and a three-inch Navy ship gun was placed on the front lawn of the Post. On April 5, 1997 the Post received a M-60 tank from Indiantown Gap. This tank was used in the Korean and Vietnam Wars to penetrate enemy defenses in order to seize or destroy vital installations. The tank weighs 50 tons and is mounted with a 105mm cannon and has a top speed of 48 km/h (30 mph).

The F-14 TomCat Jet is the most recent piece of military equipment the Post has obtained. The F-14 served in many missions during Operation Desert Shield, Operation Desert Storm and Operation Desert Fox. Following the attack on the World Trade Center, in New York, September 2001, the jet made two deployments in the International War on Terror; and was retired from flight status in September 2005. The F-14 was offered to the Richard J. Gross VFW Post and delivered on February 15, 2007 and dedicated on October 5, 2008.

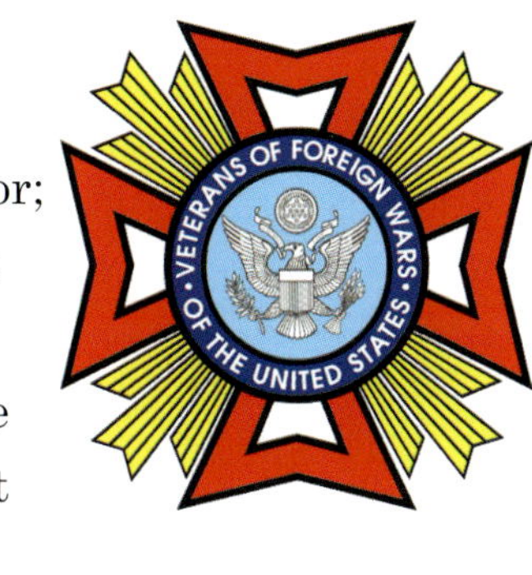

The first female veteran joined the Richard J. Gross VFW Post in July 1986, and since that time, the Post has welcomed many other female veterans.

The East Berlin Memorial Team was previously known as The Rifle Squad, which they changed their name on December 23, 1971. The team consists of a rifle squad and a color guard; they are a very special group of veterans and non-veterans who participate in the funeral services of their fallen comrades and also other memorial dedications. The outstanding merit of this team is that they give up time with their families to pay tribute to the fallen comrades. During the Memorial Day weekend, they march in the Hampton Parade on Friday night; then on Saturday they host the East Berlin Memorial Day parade. On Sunday, they travel to Stone Church in Glenville to participate in the Memorial service there, for the last 55 years. They then travel to Jefferson Cemetery and administer the military rites. They also were involved in the ceremonies at the Spring Grove VFW up until recently.

On Memorial Day, the members have breakfast and prayer at the Post Home before traveling to seven area cemeteries to pay their respects to the fallen comrades. These members are dedicated to the cause and are appreciated by many people. The Richard J. Gross VFW Post is one of the few in the area to have a Memorial team that is still very active in doing services at their fallen comrades funerals and devoting their time to honor the dead on the four-day Memorial Day weekend. We commend and thank them for their unselfish giving and dedication.

The VFW makes monthly donations to various charities, community service organizations and schools in the local area as well as participating in many school and community activities. Some of the community service activities the VFW sponsors are the Halloween party, the Easter egg hunt, blood drives, Buddy Poppy sales, flag education at the schools, Adopt a Highway (15 years), as well as the programs offered by the VFW National organization.

The Richard J. Gross VFW Post membership has grown from 283 members to 469 in 67 years.

THE LADIES AUXILIARY OF POST 8896 VETERANS OF FOREIGN WARS

was instituted at a meeting held at the Post Home on March 9, 1949, with twenty-eight charter members. The first projects completed by the Auxiliary were concerning the Post Home itself. They hung drapes and had cabinets installed in the kitchen and continued to do whatever was necessary when redecorating and dedications were held. The Auxiliary has made every effort to promote and aid in all civic affairs. They assist the Post with the community Easter egg hunt, the community Halloween party, and the Christmas party for the children of the members. Some other projects the Ladies Auxiliary participate in are Cancer projects, the Voice of Democracy essay contests, Patriot's Pen essay contest, Young American Creative Patriotic Art contest, Labor Day Poster contest, and serving banquets and weddings. The Ladies Auxiliary continues to strive to keep uppermost in their thoughts and reflect in their actions their purpose "To Honor The Dead By Remembering The Living."

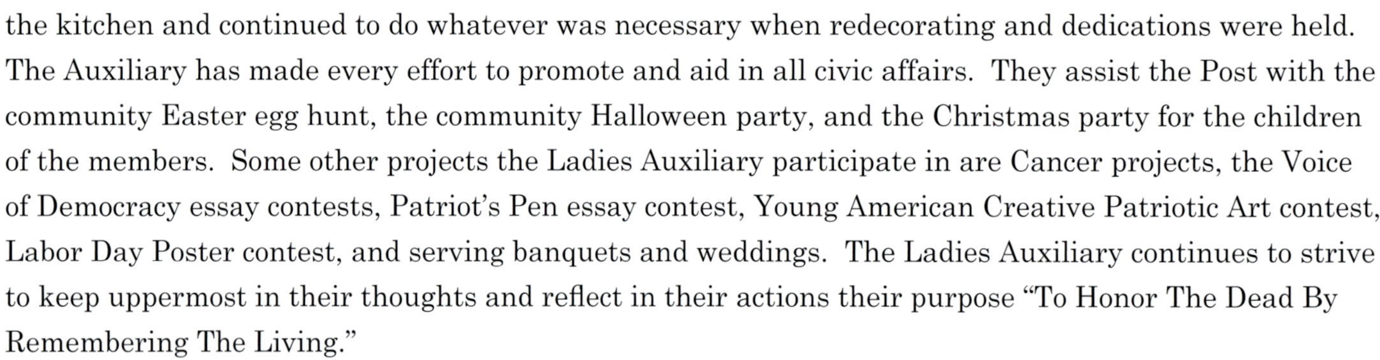

The Richard J. Gross VFW Ladies Auxiliary membership has grown from 70 members to 495 in 65 years.

The Richard J. Gross VFW and the Ladies Auxiliary have received many awards and citations from District 21, the Department of Pennsylvania and the National organization for their membership and community service efforts. The Richard J. Gross VFW and the Ladies Auxiliary work side by side on many of the community service activities and organizational programs offered. They are truly a team working to support our community, veterans, and their families past and present.

FIRE COMPANIES

Liberty Fire Company

Lake Meade Fire Company

Hampton Fire Company

BERLIN IMPROVEMENT SOCIETY 1836-1910

The Church School House, until the turn of the Twentieth Century was used for many purposes. It was the only building in town suitable for meeting at the time. The Berlin Improvement Society, established in 1836, met there for 74 years. Berlin, as the town was then known, was described as a village of 80 dwellings, five stores, three taverns and fewer than 400 persons.

The Society's main mission, as quoted in the records was "to promote the improvement of its members by reading and criticism". The members, 317 during the existence of the organization, maintained a library of over 600 volumes. The first book that was bought was Webster's Dictionary for the price of $4.50 and was promptly covered with muslin to protect it. A membership fee of 25 cents, and monthly dues of twelve and one half cents was paid by the members for the purchase of books.

Most of the books were of History, Geography, and Law and Government. They were stored in the bookcase nine feet high which was made by William J. Baugher, a local bed maker. The purchase price was $22.00 in 1842. "Education our country's pride" is inscribed on top of the case.

Forty-five honorary members were elected to the Society. Among them were two US Presidents - Buchanan and Garfield; one U.S. Vice President - George Dallas; U.S. Senators-Simon Cameron and Thaddeus Stevens.

At one period, there were no meetings recorded, from 1902 until 1906 at which time the members hoped to revive the Society by admitting high school students. The last entry in the records was 1910.

CONSTITUTION AND BYLAWS

OF THE

BERLIN IMPROVEMENT SOCIETY.

As revised, Jan. 13th. 1845.

SECTION 1.

Art. 1. The name and style of this society, shall be the Berlin Improvement Society.

Art. 2. The object of this society shall be to promote the improvement of its members by reading and criticism.

Art. 3. No person shall be admitted a member of this society, but by a vote of two thirds of the members present.

Art. 4. This society shall meet as often as may be deemed expedient, and five members shall constitute a quorum.

Art. 5. The officers of this society shall be a President, Vice President, and Secretary and Treasurer in one, who shall be elected quarterly, and if no election take place at the end of the term for which they were elected; they shall continue in office until others be elected.

Sec. 2. All elections shall be by ballot.

Art. 6. It shall be the duty of the President, or in his absence, the vice President; or in the absence of both, the chairman, (to be chosen protem.) to preside at all meetings, preserve order, appoint committees, define questions, and give a casting vote, when the members are equally divided, and appoint persons to read.

Sec. 3. Duties of the Secretary.

Art. 7. It shall be the duty of the Secretary and Treasurer, to keep accurate minutes of the proceedings of the Society; collect all fines due by members, notify all officers of their election or appointment, provide Stationary, Oil, and keep accurate accounts of the same; pay all orders drawn by the President, and exhibit to the society at the expiration of his term, a complete statement of all his receipts anddisbursements, and deliver all moneys and papers in his possession to his successor.

Sec. 4. Duties of the members.

Art. 8. Every member refusing to read when called upon by the President, shall pay a fine of six and a fourth cents, unless excused by a vote of the society.

Art. 9. Every member of this society, shall before taking his or her seat, pay twenty five cents and sign the Constitution, and pay twelve and a half cents monthly, to defray the expenses, purchase books &c.

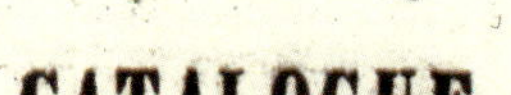

CATALOGUE,

OF THE

BOOKS,

BELONGING TO THE

BERLIN IMPROVEMENT SOCIETY.

PRINTED BY WILLIAM BART.

East Berlin, Adams County Pa.

1845

EAST BERLIN LION'S CLUB

The East Berlin Lion's Club was chartered December 12, 1957. Originally, the Lion's Club was a men's service club, and eventually they allowed women to join. The Lions Club is now comprised of men and women who volunteer their time to humanitarian causes serving the community and those less fortunate worldwide.

In 2004, the East Berlin Lion's Club opened their membership to their first female member; Hannelore (Hanna) Furst; who also became the first woman President for this club. In 2006, Hanna became the President of the East Berlin Lions Club, and held that position until 2010. The East Berlin Lion's club has added a few more women to their roster and would gladly welcome more.

The club has conducted many worthy projects over the past years. The club has co-sponsored with the York Springs Lion Club a yearly monetary award to an outstanding senior student that contributes to their community in a service project and attends the Bermudian Springs High School.

The club contributes financial support to the Beacon Lodge; which is a recreational camp for the blind; they also collect and recycle used eyeglasses to be refurbished for the under privileged countries, preventing serious vision loss for more than 30 million people worldwide.

The club also sponsors a Multiphasic Blood Screening Program, usually held the beginning of the month of June at the East Berlin Area Community Center; which helps with low cost blood screening. The Lions Club's proceeds from this event is donated to the community center.

Lion Glenn Gruver and Lion Charles Eisenhart

For many years during the Christmas season, the club has installed the seasonal lighting decorations throughout the town for the enjoyment of the citizens of the town and the surrounding communities who pass through the town. The Lion's Club purchased their copper lanterns from a local craftsman and they are displayed on the electrical poles in town. Another worthwhile project is the annual Christmas Tree Sales event held at Cashman's Hardware Store.

One of the East Berlin Lion's Club largest donation was for the new East Berlin Park; located on North Avenue. In May of 2006, the club presented a check for $20,000 for the East Berlin Community Build a Park Project. In the fall of 2011; the club held a Pig in the Park fundraiser to further support the park. The menu consisted of pulled pork sandwiches, beans, cole slaw, chips and drinks, with activities for the family, with all proceeds benefitting the park. Another Pig in the Park activity was held later in the year of 2012.

We Serve

The Lions Motto is "We Serve" and as members of this club, we are proud to serve.

The club continues to be worthwhile organization in the small town of East Berlin.

If you would like more information on how you can volunteer and become a member of our club, you can join us on the second or fourth Tuesday of each month at Zwingli Church.

EAST BERLIN COMMUNITY LIBRARY

The idea for a community library first took root in June 1975 when Reverend David Gleason, former pastor of the Trinity Lutheran Church, surveyed church members about potential service projects. The proposal to start a library got a strong response and other organizations in the area were asked to assist in its founding.

Soon after, the Trinity Lutheran Church purchased a neighboring property for use as a parish house. Two large rooms in the basement of the parish house were offered as a location for the new library at a fee of only $1.00 per month. Renovations to equip the space began shortly after the property was purchased. New shelves were constructed by John Brodbeck with lumber donated by Penn Wood Products. The East Berlin Explorer Scout Troop painted the shelves and walls with supplies donated by Cashman's Hardware Store. The Youth Corps Workers of Gettysburg catalogued donated books. Louise Pittman, then Head Librarian at the Adams County Library, gave advice and counsel to the newly formed Board of Trustees.

A boost to the project came with the celebration of Mr. and Mrs. Nevin Mummert's 50th wedding anniversary. Instead of gifts, their invitations asked for donations to the library fund. They raised

You are Cordially invited to attend
The Grand Opening of
The East Berlin Community Library
on November 23, 1975, from 2 to 4 p.m.

W. King Street
(Anna J. Stoudt)
Parish House
East Berlin, Pa.

Refreshments will be served.

Dear Friends And Members Of the Library,
Congradulations on your recent transition to the new library. I know it was the culmination of many hours of planning and work for a lot of people.
I was very happy to be able to capture A few of these moments so that you might share these memories with others now and in the future.
Please Accept this token of my appreciation.

Sincerely,
Bob Moul

$305 and donated the sum in honor of their golden wedding anniversary. A second couple, Mr. and Mrs. Lau, similarly raised contributions in honor of their 50th wedding anniversary.

The East Berlin Community Library officially opened its doors on November 23, 1975 at two o'clock in the afternoon, in the Trinity Lutheran Church parish house located at 111 West King Street. As the first order of business, Mr. and Mrs. Mummert were honored in a ceremony where they were presented with the first cards issued by the library. In total, over 100 cards were given out on the library's opening day.

In conjunction with the library, two groups were formed: the Friends of the East Berlin Library and a Board of Trustees. The Friends of the East Berlin Library held their first meeting at the Zwingli United Church of Christ on October 27, 1975. The meeting opened with the presentation of a check for $250 from Mrs. Kathy Boas, leader of the Friends Group, to Mrs. JoAnn Grim, President of the new Board of Trustees. Other members of the first Board included Vice President Linda Gleason, Treasurer Clayton Wilcox, Assistant Treasurer Ann Wilcox, Secretary Noelle Kline, Assistant Secretary Mary Grim, and Honorary Board Member Isabelle Lau.

Staffed by a team of volunteers, the library was able to offer a wide range of programs including art exhibits, children's story times, film nights, craft demonstrations, and an annual summer reading club. With the growing popularity of its programs and an increasing number of books to house, the library quickly began to outgrow the rooms of the parish house. By September of 1979, the library had over 500 members and was circulating nearly 300 books each month. At this time, the East Berlin Community Library made an agreement with the Adams County Library in Gettysburg to establish the Adams County Library System. Under this agreement, both libraries remained independent organizations, but could formally cooperate to serve patrons and share resources. That agreement continues to this day.

With a pressing need for more space, the Board approached Harold Resh who had recently

purchased the former Shetter property. Located at 109 West King Street, this lot included a house, a former restaurant, and two apartments. Resh reached an agreement with the Board allowing the the library to move into the former restaurant. The library re-opened in the new space in June 1981, under the direction of acting librarian Mary Grim. With more than triple the space of its previous location, the library now had a dedicated children's area for the first time. Mary Grim remained acting librarian until, February 1, 1982, when volunteer Elva Ward was hired to fill the position. When Elva retired in June 1984, Mary Godfriaux was brought on as the new Library Coordinator. Two years later, in 1986, Doris Walker was hired to fill the role of Librarian and would hold the position for 5 years.

The library stayed at 109 West King Street until the building was sold in 1988. At that time, the library temporarily moved into the old parsonage of the Zwingli United Church of Christ located at 405 West King Street. The library reopened Jan 3, 1989 with over 10,000 books on the shelves.

On November 11, 1991, the library opened the doors at its current location under the leadership of Director Patricia Dixon. In need of a permanent home, the library was able to acquire a former church building located at 105 Locust Street. The purchase was made possible thanks to a grant from the East Berlin Historical Society. Built in 1899, the brick structure was originally used as the meeting house for the German Baptist Brethren Church and had more recently been used as a church by the New Life Assembly of God. Extensive renovations were made to make the space suitable for a library, including a new circulation desk built by volunteer George Shaffer. In 1998, Sherry Feeser joined the library as the new Youth Services Coordinator. Under her

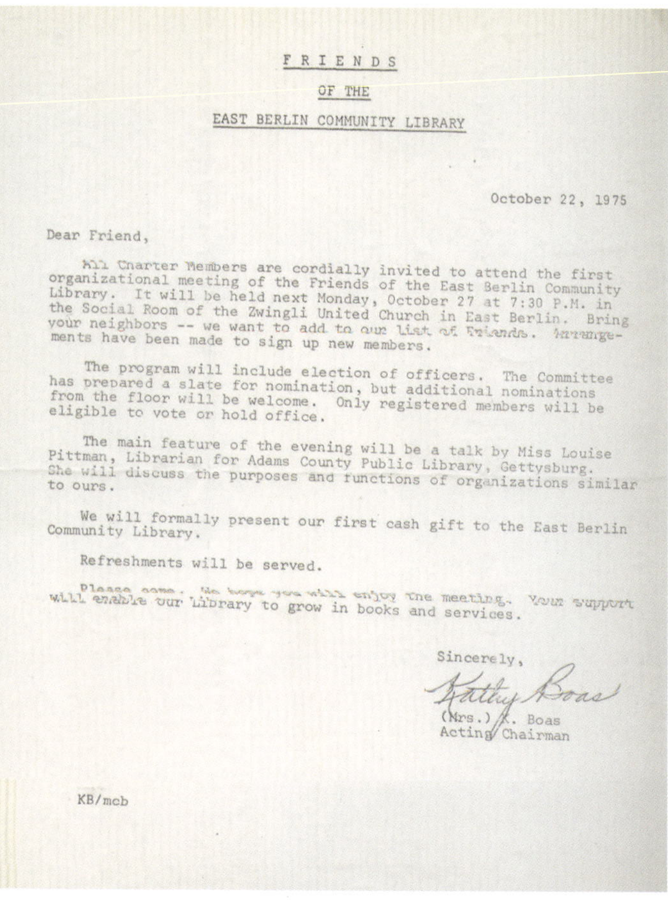

FRIENDS

OF THE

EAST BERLIN COMMUNITY LIBRARY

October 22, 1975

Dear Friend,

All Charter Members are cordially invited to attend the first organizational meeting of the Friends of the East Berlin Community Library. It will be held next Monday, October 27 at 7:30 P.M. in the Social Room of the Zwingli United Church in East Berlin. Bring your neighbors -- we want to add to our list of Friends. Arrangements have been made to sign up new members.

The program will include election of officers. The Committee has prepared a slate for nomination, but additional nominations from the floor will be welcome. Only registered members will be eligible to vote or hold office.

The main feature of the evening will be a talk by Miss Louise Pittman, Librarian for Adams County Public Library, Gettysburg. She will discuss the purposes and functions of organizations similar to ours.

We will formally present our first cash gift to the East Berlin Community Library.

Refreshments will be served.

Please come. We hope you will enjoy the meeting. Your support will enable our Library to grow in books and services.

Sincerely,

Kathy Boas

(Mrs.) K. Boas
Acting Chairman

KB/mcb

direction, the library significantly expanded its offering of children's programing and materials. In response to the increasing popularity of children's programs, Sally Caldwell was hired in 2013 as a Children's Library Associate. Sally's focus on middle school and teenage children reflects a growing need for young adult services in the community and has allowed Sherry to focus on outreach and programming services for younger children.

In 2006, the Board determined that the library's 2,300 sq. ft. was no longer large enough to accommodate the library's growing collections or the need for programming space. With increasing demand from patrons not only from East Berlin Borough, but also from Hamilton and Reading Townships, Lake Meade, and York County seeking the library's wide array of services, the East Berlin Community Library is the second busiest of the 6 libraries that make up the Adams County Library System. In 2013, the library circulated 100,570 items, making it the first branch outside of the main library in Gettysburg to circulate over 100,000 items in a calendar year.

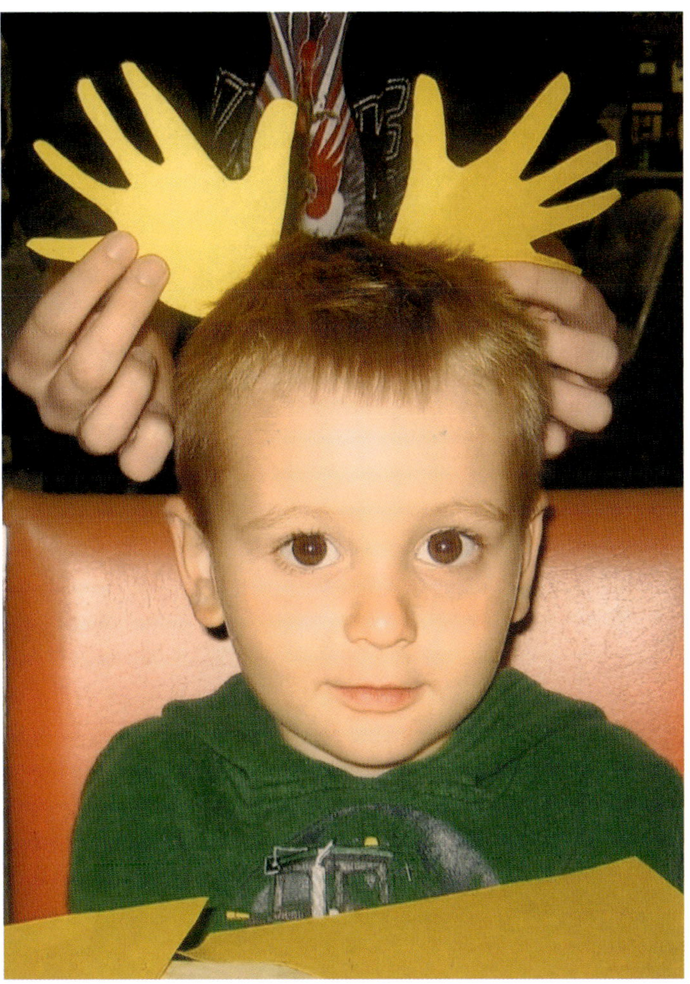

The purchase of the adjacent property at 103 Locust Street in 2010 was the first step in the plan for an expanded and renovated library that will have more than double its present size. In 2012, Brandt Ensor became the library's new Director, replacing Patricia Dixon who retired. Brandt is the library's first director with a master's degree in library science as well as the first, and currently only, full-time employee. Brandt has organized and led the library's capital campaign with the help of the current Board of Trustees: President Sandra Abnett, Linda Gawthrop, Robert Greer III, M.D., Barbara McCarthy Greer, Patricia Campbell, Marion Mitchell, Sharry Gresens, Wayne Ogburn, and Rev. Don Mitchell.

When the project is realized, the library will have private study rooms, separate wings for adult and children, and a teen zone designed for young adults. This new building will better match the needs of today's users, including better accessibility and upgraded equipment and furnishings.
With the hiring of Kyla O'Hara as the new Adult Services Librarian in 2014, there are currently two professional librarians on the library's six-person staff. In addition to those named above, Cathy Horn has served the library for over 18 years as a Library Associate and Carrie Hamm joined the staff as a Library Associate for Adult Services in 2013. Working alongside the library's regular staff, a team of dedicated volunteers generously give their time to help process and shelve materials.

As the East Berlin Community Library looks to its future, we have been honored to serve the community and remain dedicated to meeting the diverse needs of our patrons and the community that we live in. Congratulations East Berlin Borough on 250 years!

THE HISTORY OF EAST BERLIN BOROUGH HALL

The Borough Hall that is located at 128 Water Street is a recent addition to the town. Prior to its construction in 1975, the Town Council and Mayor would meet in the second floor of the old Fire Hall located on Fourth Street. The meetings at the old Fire House would at times be disrupted with the sounds of bats scurrying about the upper levels of the building. Items that were kept from the old location are an old slant front desk and the curved oak chairs that are still used in the council meeting room today.

The current location was chosen because it would be located next to the sewer plant on land already owned by the Borough. A grant from the State in the amount of $64,000.00 was given to the Borough to build the current Borough Hall. The construction cost were kept to the amount of $64,000.00 due to the electrical, interior, and plumbing work done by borough employees Mike Thoman and Lynn Slothour. All original minute books and ordinances dating from 1764 are kept in a vault for safe keeping. The old maps that are hanging in the back of the borough council meeting room are dated 1884.

EAST BERLIN AREA COMMUNITY CENTER (EBACC)

In the late 1980's, the Bermudian Springs School District made the decision to put elementary, middle, and high school students on one campus. Community-minded residents of East Berlin initiated a movement to purchase the former elementary and high school building and convert the building and grounds into a community center. The small committee consisting of Joanne Eisenhart, Charlie Hoffman, and others held meetings in Joanne's kitchen to organize this effort in 1990. The school district vacated the premises in December of 1990. After negotiations with the Bermudian Springs School District, the current building and surrounding property was purchased for $125,000 in cooperation with the East Berlin Borough, and the East Berlin Area Community Center (EBACC) was born.

The building and grounds are owned by the East Berlin Borough and managed by a board of directors. The board of directors is comprised of two representatives from the six municipalities that are served by EBACC; East Berlin Borough, Abbottstown Borough, Hamilton Township, Paradise Township, Reading Township, and Washington Township. The board of directors creates the strategic vision and long-range goals for EBACC working in conjunction with the surrounding municipalities.

EBACC has been primarily managed and operated by volunteers, who have organized events, cleaned, completed repairs, raised funds, conducted classes and programs and much more. In 1995, a community thrift shoppe was opened by Warren and Peggy Frey. Warren also served on the board of directors as a representative from Washington Township. Peggy Frey and several volunteers sorted donations, priced the items, and sold them at the shoppe. The thrift shoppe has now expanded to include a biannual book sale, a Christmas shoppe in December, and six clearance sales held each year. Over 40 volunteers help to sort, price, display, and staff the thrift shoppe. The thrift shoppe has now become one of the largest fundraisers for EBACC.

Warren Frey also started a children's basketball program in 1992 where youth aged 5-16 learn skills and play games over an 8-week period in the gymnasium. The program has been extremely successful, and in recent years attendance has been limited to ensure that every child has the opportunity to play and learn.

The EBACC Fitness Center opened in January 2000 and features a fully equipped workout facility. Personal training is provided for members as awareness in healthy lifestyles increases. The outside grounds have been improved with the assistance of VFW Post 8896 with a new pavilion and outdoor grill. Many reunions, birthday parties, graduation celebrations, and picnics are held throughout the year. Two baseball fields are available and a sand volleyball court was installed for community enjoyment. Playground equipment has been installed for youth and those young at heart to enjoy.

A senior center serves hot meals during the week and provides a place for older citizens to congregate and socialize. Summer camps featuring sports, cooking, arts, dance, theater, and more are offered every year for our younger generation. Adult programs such as yoga, Zumba, forensic science, watercolor and more are offered to serve the surrounding communities. In 2013, the kitchen was totally reconditioned, and it is now a fully commercial licensed facility. This enables EBACC to cater events such as weddings, birthday parties, corporate functions, and more.

EBACC continues to engage and work with the surrounding municipalities to build a stronger community.

MEMORABILIA

THINGS TO REMEMBER

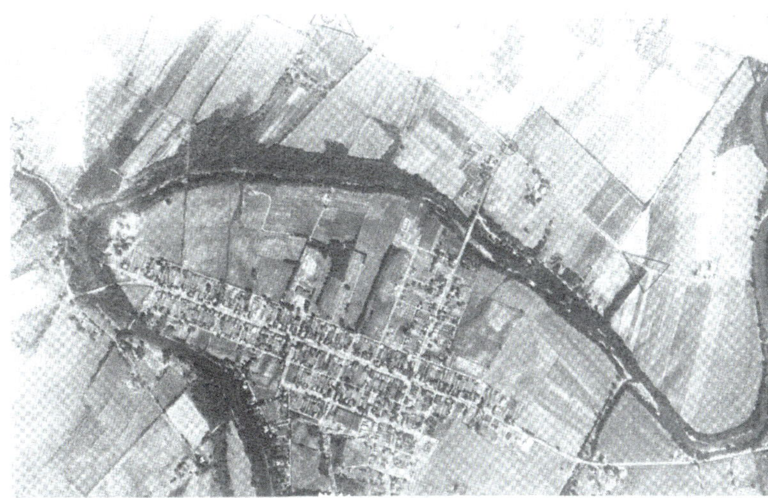

Bird's Eye View of East Berlin in 1907.

Flood — House — Mill

The Flood of 1933.

Repairing the Dam in 1963.

A Product of the Conewago

The pride of the Community; the original "heated outhouse."

Redmen's Parade of 1917

Returning from a picnic, we watch the birdie.

H. H. WALLACE — HARNESS AND SHOE REPAIRING — CIGARS, TOBACCO AND CONFECTIONERY

In this community "fix-it" shop, dating to 1894 and before, H. H. Wallace made and repaired shoes, made and repaired harness. Perhaps the customer needed a haircut — 10¢ or a shave — 5¢. If a bucket needed mending, a pulley needed a new cover or a rope needed splicing, the door to the shop welcomed the distressed caller. Many a breakdown or emergency was repaired promptly by this "Jack-of-all-Trades." The shop has been relocated recently.

The bridge at Ducky-Wucky

East Berlin firemen help a neighbor's parade.

Aerial view of Mummert's Grove Bridge.

The old wooden draw well.

The annual New Year's Day horse sale.

"Fat" Miller's Cigar Store.

Cream Separator's Demonstration

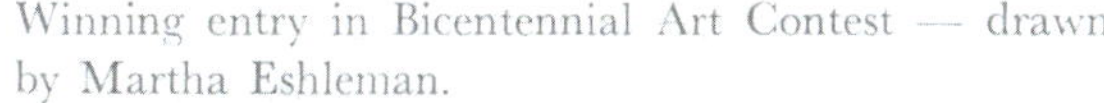

Winning entry in Bicentennial Art Contest — drawn by Martha Eshleman.

Max Darone: In appreciation of his many and varied contributions to our Bicentennial.

EAST BERLIN BICENTENNIAL 1964

EAST BERLIN BICENTENNIAL

JUNE 14-20

1964

BICENTENNIAL COMMITTEES

EXECUTIVE COMMITTEE

Irwin Gross, General Chairman
Helen Altland, Secretary
C. L. Spangler, Treasurer

Rosella Altland
Alfred Billett
Melvin Eisenhart
Eugene Elgin
Russell Fissell
Sylvia Herman
Hazel Hoffman
John Kohler
Mary Krall
Kurvin Krout
Robert Lau
Mary Markley
Dr. John Schwartz
Charles B. Wallace

HISTORICAL PUBLICATION DIVISION

ADVERTISING COMMITTEE

Irwin Gross, Chairman

Harry Albert
Roy Chronister
Louise Eisenhart
Ruth Frey
Ralph Hoffacker
Carlton Jacobs
Robert Lau
Ira Lobaugh
Raymond Miller
Richard Smyers

HISTORICAL COMMITTEE

(HISTORICAL DATA AND DISPLAYS)

Charles B. Wallace, Chairman

Dorothy Eisenhart
Kathryn Eisenhart
Charles Gentzler
M. Florence Gentzler
Isabel Lau
Arthur Leas
Jeune Leas
Charles Philips
Ethel Resser
Edith Reynolds
Lloyd Wagener
Glenn Weaver
Mae Wolf

PUBLICATION COMMITTEE

Alfred R. Billett, Chairman

Martha Eshleman
Wayne Lau
Gary Markley
John Rebert
Lloyd Wagener
Charles B. Wallace

SUBSCRIPTIONS AND CIRCULATION COMMITTEE

Eugene Elgin, Chairman

Larry Fissel
Charlotte Glatfelter
Marilyn Hoover
Leonard Myers

SPECIALTIES DIVISION

FIREWORKS COMMITTEE

Kurvin Krout, Chairman

John Lerew
Lloyd Chronister

PAGEANT COMMITTEE

Hazel Hoffman, Chairman

Ruth Frey
Wayne Lau
Arthur Leas
William Lerew
Romaine Myers
Melissa Roos
Rebecca Weaver

PARADE COMMITTEE

Melvin Eisenhart, Chairman

Earl Bollinger
David Krout

PARTICIPATION DIVISION

BICENTENNIAL BELLES COMMITTEE

Mary Markley, Chairman

Lois Eisenhart
Ruth Lusk
Carolyn Mummert
Joyce Shafer
Lelia Sowards
Ruth Spangler

BROTHERS OF THE BRUSH COMMITTEE

Russell Fissel, Chairman

Lester Chronister
Lloyd Chronister
Paul Fahs
Elvin Lau

QUEEN CONTEST COMMITTEE

Sylvia Herman, Chairman

Marie Adam
Treva Chronister
Janet Sheffer

REVENUE DIVISION

FINANCE COMMITTEE

C. L. Spangler, Chairman

E. R. Altland
Lloyd Chronister
Dr. Joseph Eshleman
Raymond Hoffman
Raymond Jacobs
Sherman Krall
Wayne Lau
Paul Lerew
Cletus Mummert
Richard Smyers

FOOD COMMITTEE

Mary Krall, Chairman

Ethel Altland
Alice Altland
Frances Crone
Margaret Eisenhart
Kathryn Eisenhart
Nettie Gochenour
Ruth Gentzler
Ella Green
Carolyn Mummert
Jean Spangler
Jean Wisler
Ruthanna Wallace

NOVELTIES COMMITTEE

Rosella Altland, Chairman

Richard Herman
Sylvia Herman
Gene Swartz
Helen Altland
Rudolph Altland

ADDITIONAL COMMITTEES

PARKING AND TRAFFIC COMMITTEE

John Kohler, Chairman

Robert Lusk
Howard Shafer
William Shafer
Harvey Spangler

PROGRAM COMMITTEE

Dr. John Schwartz, Chairman

Othmar Carli
Irwin Gross
Hazel Hoffman
Isabel Lau
Arthur Leas
Elmer Miller
Harry Manning
Katharine Manning

PUBLICITY COMMITTEE

Helen Altland, Chairman

Ernest Adam
Marie Adam
Rudolph Altland
Richard Herman
Sylvia Herman
Charles Reynolds

GENERAL LIGHTING

Roy Boyer

The above lists of names appear here as submitted by the various committees.

SUNDAY

Sunday Morn

The Choir

Checking equipment

Platform speakers and guests

Dr. Schwartz, Mr. VanZandt, Mr. Goodling, Mr. Hawbaker, Mr. Ridinger, Judge Sheely.

The Cakewalk

MONDAY

READY FOR THE JUDGES

MOTHER AND DAUGHTER WINNERS

Mrs. Paul Wolf and Daughter

Mrs. Charles Fetrow and Daughter

V

Bicentennial Queen

Queen Patricia Graybill is crowned by Adams County Apple Blossom Queen, Martha McDannell. Runner-up, Linda Rohrbaugh; crown bearers, Bart Frey and Holly Sheffer.

Queen of the Belles
Queen Pamela Eisenhart receives trophy from Mistress of Ceremonies, Lizzie Gary Davis.

THE BROTHERS OF THE BRUSH

TUESDAY

Square Dancers

Pet Show Grand Champion — Lisa Slothour

Indian Dancers

Cakewalk

WEDNESDAY

Dedication of Time Capsule

List of probable items to be placed in the Time Capsule located beneath the memorial stone on the lawn of the Richard J. Gross Post #8896, Veterans of Foreign Wars: V.F.W. materials, aerial map of the town, Bicentennial letterhead and envelope, commemorative cancellation stamp, commemorative coin, guide to exhibits, menu, program of elementary pageant — *Life of Stephen Foster,* program of Bicentennial Pageant — *The Plow and the Sword,* parade-prize list, schedule of events, *Wheels of Time* and supplement, other Bicentennial souvenirs as will fit the container.

I would like to open my brief remarks by paraphrasing a statement once made by Daniel Webster, the famous New Englander. He was referring to Dartmouth College in these words; It is a small college but there are those who love it. *I would like to make the same statement about East Berlin: It is a small town, but there are those who love it. And I suppose that in these recent months of preparation and in this week of celebration, we are finding out that there are many, perhaps many more than we realized, who love East Berlin.*

What is happening this week is more than a celebration. It goes far deeper than that. Certainly it is a cradle of memories of the many events which have taken place in the past two hundred years; but equally important, what is happening here is something of a rebirth, a springboard into the future. — Max Darone

EAST BERLIN ELEMENTARY PAGEANT

THURSDAY

PENNSYLVANIA STATE POLICE
RODEO

IX

FRIDAY

Camp Entrance

Camp

Indians

Drum and Fife

BICENTENNIAL PAGEANT

THE PLOW AND THE SWORD

SATURDAY

THE PARADE

1920
SCOUTING IN EAST BERLIN 1912
1912
1959

WEST
234

LIGHT LUNCH & PIZZA
Coca-Cola
Little Colonials

234

PREPARING FOR THE CELEBRATION

All forms of transportation lead to the Bicentennial Headquarters and Studebaker House.

Governor Pinchot's Studebaker

DISPLAY IN STUDEBAKER HOUSE

CRAFTS' DISPLAY

CANDLEMAKING
WOOD AND BONE ORIGINALS
QUILTING AND TATTING

Steam Engine Display

Art Display

The Berlin Beneficial Society chartered in 1844 met monthly in the *Church School House*. None but citizens of the United States between the ages of twenty-one and forty-five, free from all disease and infirmity were admitted as members. Two overseers were appointed by the President for a period of two months. It was their duty to collect twenty-five cents from the members at each stated meeting and pay the same to the treasurer, to visit the sick or infirmed members if within four miles of the meeting place within eighteen hours; and if within two miles, to visit every third day. No member became a Beneficiary of the Association until one year after he signed the Constitution. Sick benefits were $3.50 per week if bedfast, $2.50 per week if of a less serious nature. Death benefits were $25.

And so, the question, *Am I My Brother's Keeper?* was answered then as it can be answered today, *Yes, I am; and I am also My Brother's Brother.*

CHARTER,

CONSTITUTION,

AND

BY-LAWS,

OF

THE BERLIN BENEFICIAL SOCIETY.

Chartered December, 10th. 1844.

EAST-BERLIN:

PRINTED BY WM. BART.

184[illegible]

ANTIQUE DISPLAY

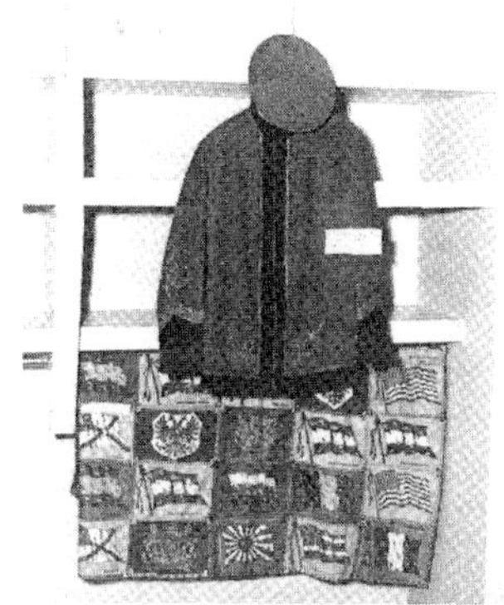

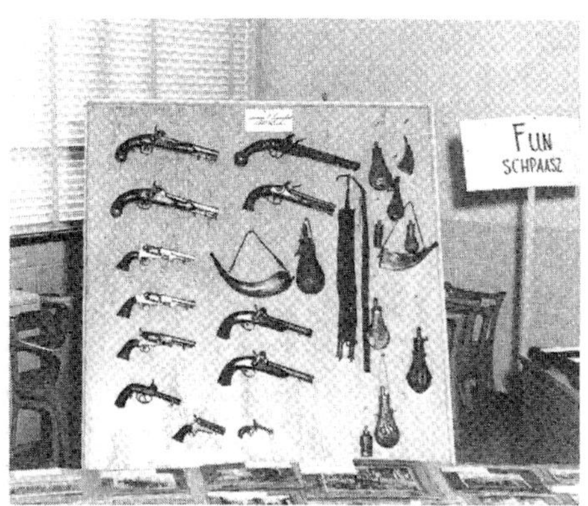

Mrs. Gentzler displays some of her antiques.

ONE DOLLAR

EAST BERLIN BICENTENNIAL COMMISSION

EAST BERLIN, PENNSYLVANIA

THIS CERTIFIES THAT Willy Brandt is the owner of One Shares of Common Stock of

IN WITNESS WHEREOF, the said Corporation has caused this Certificate to be signed by its duly authorized officers

the 3rd day of September 1963

Treasurer

President

Mayor Willy Brandt of *Berlin*, Germany, recognizes our Bicentennial.

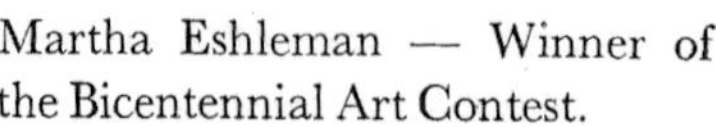

Martha Eshleman — Winner of the Bicentennial Art Contest.

XIX

CHURCH SCHOOL HOUSE

CIRCA 1769

The *Church School House* was built in 1769 to be used by the community for various purposes. Its original construction of log, stone and mud was covered at a later date with clapboard siding. The building has been used as a church, school, and meeting place for many organizations in the community. The East Berlin Improvement Society and the Beneficial Society were born in this building in 1836 and 1844 respectively. The Borough Council held its meetings in this building at its inception in 1879. For many years, it was used as a polling place for the elections in the Borough.

The East Berlin Lions Club, with the cooperation of the Union Cemetery Trustee Board and the help of many organizations and individuals, has renovated this building to the degree in which it is found today. Restoration will continue; and some day, the *Church School House* may be restored to its original form of logs and mud. As history grows, so will the community's pride in this historical site.

XX

THE JAIL

Town Officials

The night was dark,
The jail was gone.
Youth left its mark
Of ashes on lawn.

Young faces were flush,
And wallets depleted.
With braun and a rush
A new jail was completed.

For fun its use
From clergy to faker,
And seldom abuse
To Sheriff Baker.

Getting Lecture

What did Rev. Stoudt do?

Our visiting dignitaries

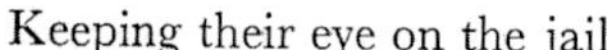

Keeping their eye on the jail

The cooks return from jail

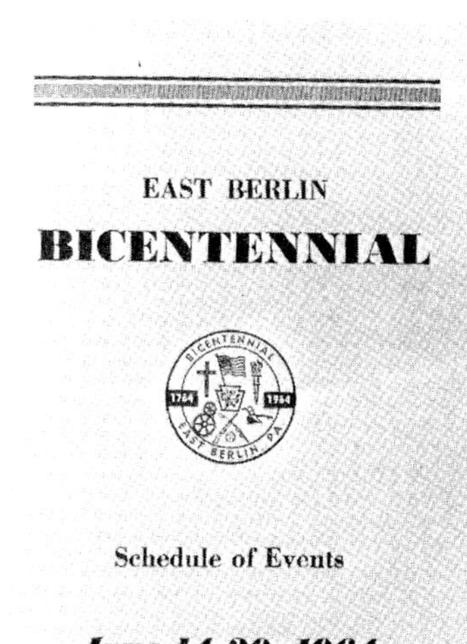

EAST BERLIN

BICENTENNIAL

Schedule of Events

June 14-20, 1964

SUNDAY, JUNE 14

Morning—Individual Church Service Observances

3:00 P.M.—Elementary School Grounds—Flag Day Observance
Invocation—Rev. William Anderman
National Anthem
Introduction of Honored Guests
Messages
Community Choir—Anthem: "Born to Be Free"
Keynote Address—Mr. James E. VanZandt
Special Representative of the Governor
Community Choir—Anthem: "Battle Hymn of Republic"
Prayer—Elder Bruce Anderson
Benediction—Rev. Harold Stoudt

5:00 P.M.—Band Concert—Bermudian Springs High School Band
Review of Queen Contestants—in costume
Ice Cream Social

☆ ☆ ☆

MONDAY, JUNE 15

7:00 P.M.—Elementary School Grounds
Barbershop Singing—The Penn-aires
Judging of Bicentennial Belles
Judging of Bicentennial Queen
Judging of Brothers of the Brush

9:30 P.M.—Elementary School Auditorium—The Queen's Ball

☆ ☆ ☆

TUESDAY, JUNE 16

2:00 P.M.—Elementary School Parking Area
Judging of Pet Contest—Many Prizes

7:00 P.M.—Elementary School Grounds
Square Dance Exhibition—The Cannonaders
Group participation in Square Dancing
Authentic Plains Indian Dancing—York Tribe

Between the Acts

Let's get started

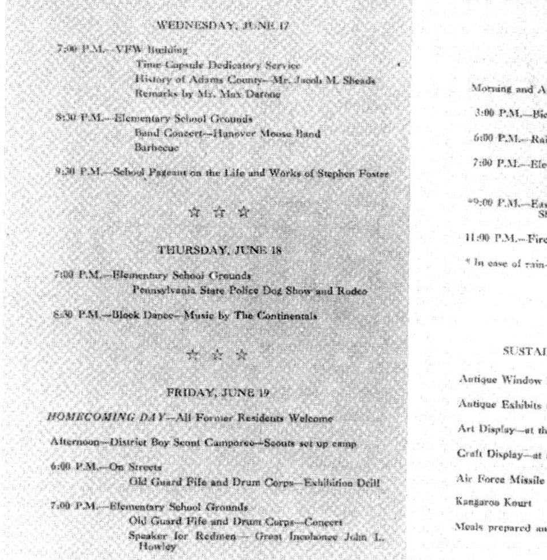

WEDNESDAY, JUNE 17

7:00 P.M.—VFW Building
Time Capsule Dedicatory Service
History of Adams County—Mr. Jacob M. Sheads
Remarks by Mr. Max Darone

8:30 P.M.—Elementary School Grounds
Band Concert—Hanover Moose Band
Barbecue

9:30 P.M.—School Pageant on the Life and Works of Stephen Foster

☆ ☆ ☆

THURSDAY, JUNE 18

7:00 P.M.—Elementary School Grounds
Pennsylvania State Police Dog Show and Rodeo

8:30 P.M.—Block Dance—Music by The Continentals

☆ ☆ ☆

FRIDAY, JUNE 19

HOMECOMING DAY—All Former Residents Welcome

Afternoon—District Boy Scout Camporee—Scouts set up camp

6:00 P.M.—On Streets
Old Guard Fife and Drum Corps—Exhibition Drill

7:00 P.M.—Elementary School Grounds
Old Guard Fife and Drum Corps—Concert
Speaker for Redmen — Great Incohonee John L. Howley

*9:00 P.M.—East Berlin Pageant—"The Plow and the Sword"—First Showing

SATURDAY, JUNE 20

Morning and Afternoon—Inspection of Scouting Displays

3:00 P.M.—Bicentennial Parade

6:00 P.M.—Rain Time for Parade

7:00 P.M.—Elementary School Grounds
Band Concert—Bermudian Springs High School Band

*9:00 P.M.—East Berlin Pageant—"The Plow and the Sword"—Final Showing

11:00 P.M.—Fireworks Display

* In case of rain—Pageant will be given Sunday, June 21.

☆ ☆ ☆

SUSTAINING EVENTS DURING THE WEEK

Antique Window Displays

Antique Exhibits throughout the town

Art Display—at the Square

Craft Display—at the Square

Air Force Missile Exhibit

Kangaroo Kourt

Meals prepared and served at the Elementary School Cafeteria

Antiquity fades, but not into oblivion — Doctor Wolf's Drug Store

The strong arm of the law found a weak end at the end of the week.

Eternal God of our fathers in ages past, be with us yet, lest we forget that it was their faith and trust in Thee that brought us to this hour.

In faith they wrought; in faith they sacrificed; in faith they achieved. In their holy trust in Thee they grew spiritually strong and materially comfortable.

May we, today, take note that they were men and women who with their children walked close to Thee and worshipped Thee.

Help us throughout this bicentennial week to rededicate our lives to this same faith and trust in Thee. May we apply our hearts unto instruction and our ears to words of Knowledge and understanding.

We thank Thee for allowing the plans for this bicentennial to mature and become a reality. May this week go down in history long to be remembered for personal good realized, and may honor and glory come to Thy great name. May this community be drawn together in a greater measure of love and respect for one another.

God bless the church, the school, the civic organizations, the business establishments, together with those who till the soil. Bless and reward well the various committees and personnel who labored so earnestly to make this bicentennial possible. God bless our great state and nation. May peace and good will rule and reign.

Then when we have well spent this week, grant each one of us that holy restlessness wherein we will never be satisfied with our present achievements, but may each one of us ever press on to be perfect men and women in Jesus Christ, in whose name we have prayed. Amen — Elder Bruce Anderson's prayer of June 14, 1964.

. . . This year marks the 200th anniversary of the founding of East Berlin; and this day, June 14, marks the 187th anniversary of the Stars and Stripes as the flag of our country.

The story of East Berlin is as typically American as Flag Day. It is the story of men and women — many of whose names are unknown to us — with a vision of American destiny and a will to convert that vision into reality . . .

It represents those ideals of liberty, truth, and justice that motivated the pioneer settlers in East Berlin, and toward which we must continue to strive.

Ladies and gentlemen, it is this heritage which we must pass on to future generations. As true Americans we can do no less . . . Excerpts from the opening address of the Honorable James Van Zandt given Sunday, June 14, 1964.

STUDEBAKER LOTS

This Indenture made the 8th day of July 1790 between Marilles Comfort and Christiana Close, Executors of the last will and testament of Andrew Comfort, Senior, of Berwick Twp. in York County, deceased, on the first part, and David Studebaker of Paradise Twp, York Co., on the second part, purchased from Marilles Comfort and Christiana Close for consideration of 5 shilling lawful money truly in hand paid by said David Studebaker, his heirs and assigns, the described front lots of ground in the town of Berlin, known on the general plan of said town by numbers 13 and 14, situated on the south side of King Street, each lot containing in breadth on said street 65 ft., in depth 220 ft. to an alley, bounded with lot #15 on the street.

General Chairman of the Bicentennial, Irwin Gross, receives a quilt made and presented to him by his sister, Florence Hull. Mary Hull assists in the display of the quilt.

CURTIS EISENHART

ıne town has been strengthened through the quiet but sincere interest and unselfish devotion of Curtis Eisenhart, born May 28, 1888 at Eisenhart's Mill in Washington Township, York County, Pennsylvania.

"Curt," as he is known by his friends, was elected to Borough Council in 1946 and served until 1957. During that time, he has served faithfully on the following committees: ordinance, water, street and sanitation.

Since 1957, he has been Borough Secretary. His keen sense of historical happenings is an invaluable aid to the councilmen.

His early life, approximately a half century, was spent as a miller. He is married to the former Nellie Hoff. They are the parents of eight children.

The strength of America lies in the heart of its citizens. Here, too, lies the strength of our community. Never before in the peace-time history of our community has it poured out its heart to others as it did during the preparation and celebration of our Bicentennial.

There were many values received from the Bicentennial: individual pride, beautification of the town, renewal of old acquaintances. Perhaps the greatest value received was the uniting of the people in the community. Few, if any, took no part in the celebration. Organizations and individuals united their talents and efforts in a common cause that spelled success.

Financially, the Bicentennial Commission realized a profit of approximately $5000. With the anticipated aid of Project 70 and through the Borough Council, this money is being used to help with the purchase and erection of the Kuhn Memorial Park. Through the generosity of the Kuhn Estate, 36 acres of land, mostly wooded area on the west side of town bordering Abbottstown Street and extending to the Conewago Creek, will constitute the park site. This will be a living testimony of the significance of man in our community in this year of our Lord, 1964.

EAST BERLIN NEW YEAR CELEBRATION 2014

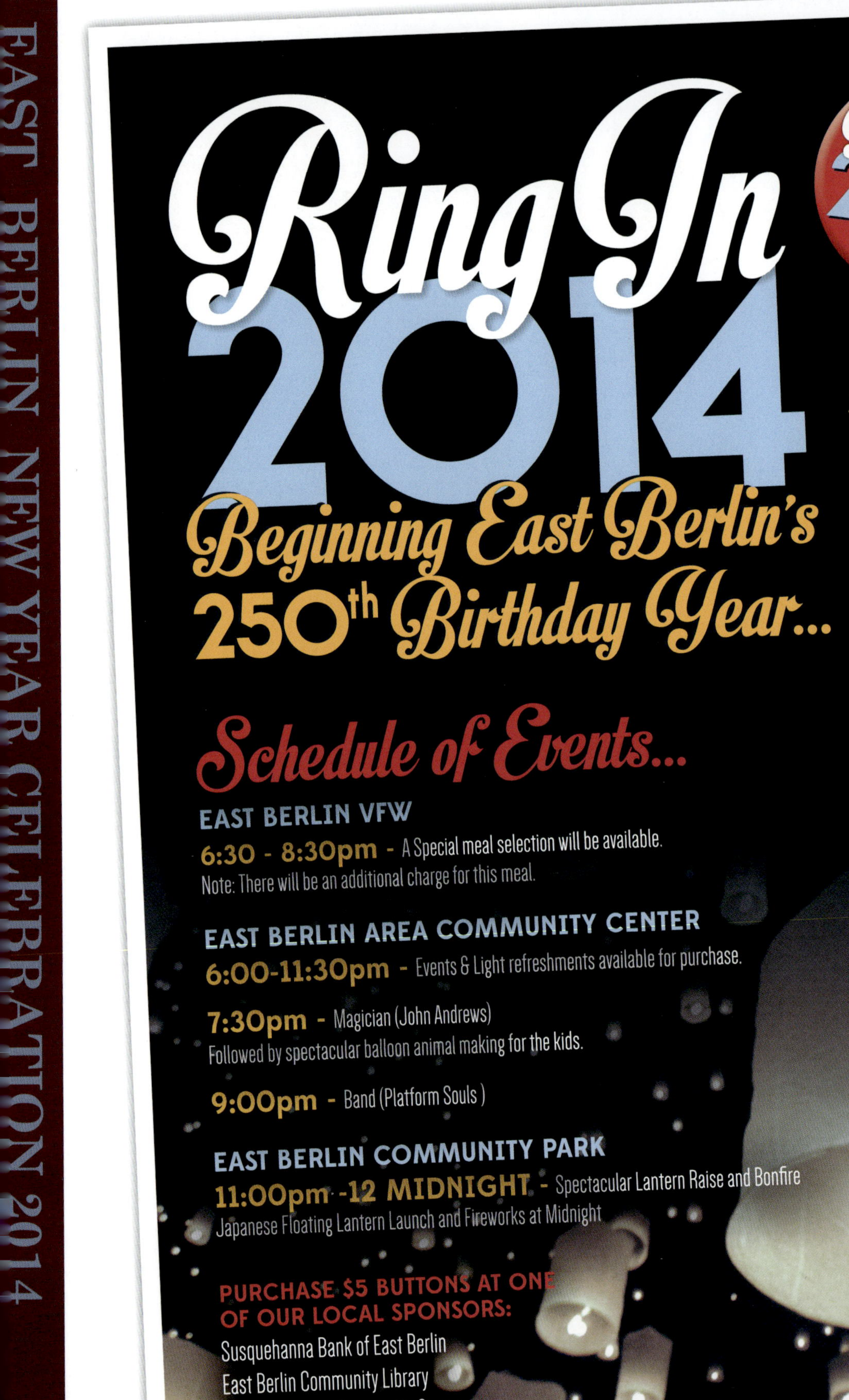

DSKINS

JLG LIFT

Commemorative GIFTS Available!!
FOUNDERS DAY COMMITTEE
Celebrating 250 Years of East Berlin
Calendars } $15.00
Wines } $15.00
Glassware } $8.00

ANTIQUE SHOW • PARADE • OLD-TIME COMMUNITY CARNIVAL • COMMUNITY SUPPER
FOOD • LIVE MUSIC • DANCING • PRESENTATIONS • REENACTORS • HISTORY TOURS

In May 2014, East Berlin with celebrate its 250th Anniversary. Founded by John Frankenberger on May 8th 1764, the town is planning a series of events to commemorate this once in a life-time occurrence. The following is a list of special events planned for the week of May 1-11 2014.

1764 - 2014

Come and join in on the merriment.

List of Events

MAY 1ST -3RD:
Historic East Berlin Antique Show presented by the East Berlin Historical Preservation Society being held at the East Berlin Area Community Center 405 North Ave.

MAY 3RD 5:00 P.M.:
A parade featuring the Old Guard Fife and Drum Corps, from W. King St to south on Abbottstown St. ending at the East Berlin VFW where there will be a brief ceremonial blessing of the town and the opening of the 1964 Time Capsule.

MAY 4TH: 1:00-4:00 P.M.:
An Old-time Community Carnival with food, pony rides and games for the enjoyment of people of all ages at the East Berlin Community Center (EBACC) from 1:00-4:00.

MAY 4TH 7:00 P.M.:
Community Chorus will perform at Trinity Lutheran Church at 117 W. King St.

MAY 6TH AND 7TH:
Two settings for Supper at 5:30 and 7:00 will be held at East Berlin Area Community Center. Followed by a walking history and mystery tour of historic west end of East Berlin. Walking tour time is approximately 6:15 and 7:45 p.m. Come and enjoy Dinner, Death and Dastardly Details. Dinner cost $10.00. Tour cost $15.00, children under 12 years old tour tickets are $10.00. Call 259-0513, 259-8848 or 259-9000 for reservations for dinner and Tour tickets.

MAY 8TH:
Happy Birthday East Berlin! The East Berlin Post Office and the East Berlin Historical Preservation Society will offer a special pictorial cancellation imprint from 9:00 a.m. till 1:00 p.m. at the Old Fire Hall, 101 Fourth Street. There will be a Dinner, cost of $15.00 with Birthday Cake at the East Berlin Area Community Center starting at 6:00 p.m. Musical entertainment provided by Lake Meade Orchestra at 7:15 and there will be Fireworks at the park after dusk approximately 9:00 p.m. Call 259-0513 or 259-8848 for reservations for dinner.

MAY 10TH AND 11TH:
East Berlin will be invaded by General Jubal Early's Confederate 2nd Corps as they were during the Civil War. The 80-100 Confederate soldiers, 10-12 horses and one cannon will camp near the East Berlin Community Park on North Ave. Living History Speakers will give presentations on life during the "Northern Aggression" from 9:00 a.m. till 1:00 p.m. General Jubal Early's troops will capture the town at 1:00 pm and there will be a skirmish at 2:00 p.m. on the 10th and the 11th. A Civil War dance from 7:00 – 10:00 will be held at the pavilion in the park. Tickets for the dance are $10.00 per person or $15.00 per couple. To end the week of celebration on May 11, at 10:00 there will be a Civil War Era Church Service at the pavilion.

Parade May 3, 2014

Richard Fox as Benjamin Franklin

Sandy & Randy Frankenberger, Grand Marshalls & decendents of our original Founding Father John Frankenberger. In a replica Victorian wedding carriage pulled by horses Carla and Cindy.

U.S. Army Old Fife & Drum Corp.

State Rep. Will Tallman joins Adams County Commissioner Jim Martin in the parade. In a 1964 Galaxy 500 convertable driven by Todd Eichelberger

Kevin Grim & son on their John Deere tractor

East Berlin Tour May 6 + 7, 2014

Storyteller Ann Griffith gave a historical tour of East Berlin including the Old School House.

Dinner Concert May 8, 2014

Civil War Reenactment May 10 + 11, 2014

A lady, deep in thought, at the Sunday Civil War church service

General Doubleday

In Progress: The arresting of the Borough Council Members: Left to Right James LeVan, Robbie Teal, Charles Krall

2ND SOUTH CAROLINA
STRING BAND
MUSICIAN'S
2nd

1964 Original Pages

Left to right: Lloyd Wagener, John Rebert, Alfred Billett, Charles Wallace.

To the community we present *The Wheels of Time* on the occasion of our Bicentennial anniversary, this year of our Lord, 1964.

We are hopeful that the results of the many hours of tedious labor may be viewed with pleasure and acceptance.

THE STAFF

EDITOR .... *Alfred R. Billett*
Assistant Editor .... *John A. Rebert*
Historical Committee
Chairman .... *Charles B. Wallace*
Photography Editor .... *Alfred R. Billett*
Assistant Photography
Editor .... *Gary L. Markley*
Art Editor .... *Lloyd W. Wagener*
Assistant Art Editor .... *Martha J. Eshleman*
Business Manager .... *Wayne E. Lau*

PATRONS

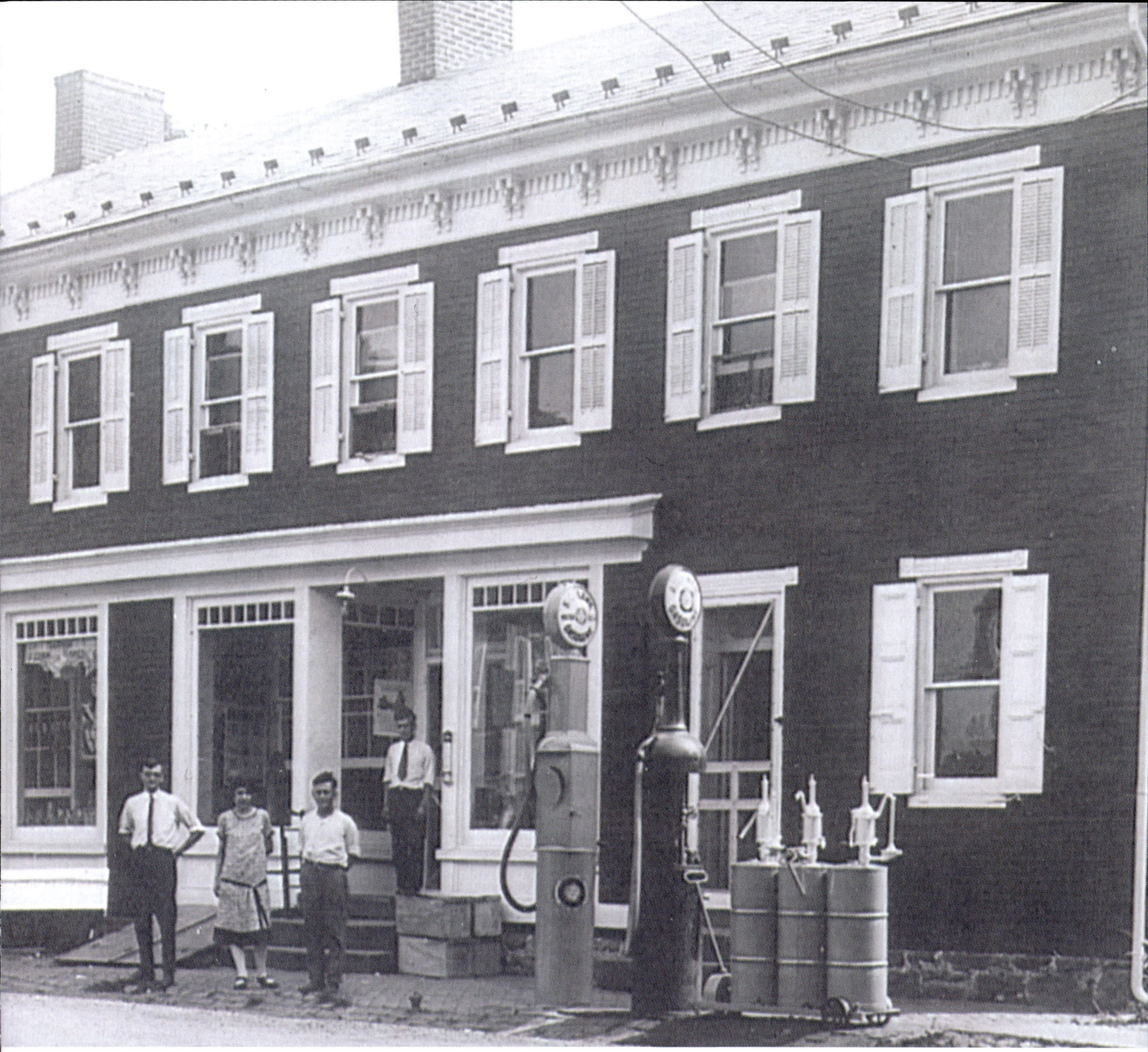

A gas station from days gone by in East Berlin, Pennsylvania.

C. 1769

Education

built 1794

Historic East Berlin

Conservation

built 1892

Preservation

East Berlin Historical Preservation Society

Post Office Box 73, 332 W. King Street
East Berlin, PA 17316
(717) 259-0822
Email: ebhps@comcast.net
www.ebhpspa.org

built 1832

built 1840

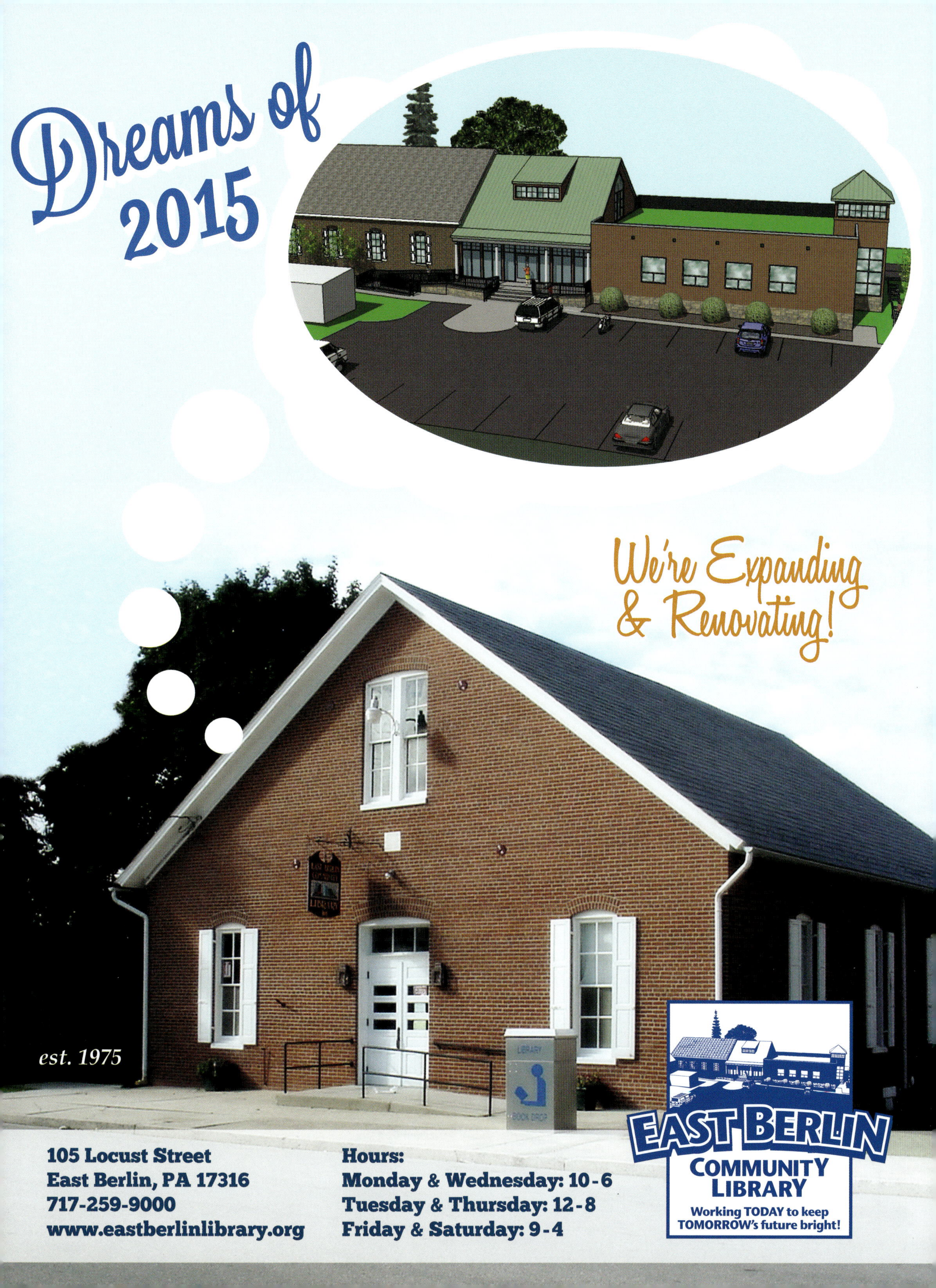
Dreams of 2015
We're Expanding & Renovating!
est. 1975
105 Locust Street
East Berlin, PA 17316
717-259-9000
www.eastberlinlibrary.org
Hours:
Monday & Wednesday: 10 - 6
Tuesday & Thursday: 12 - 8
Friday & Saturday: 9 - 4
EAST BERLIN
COMMUNITY LIBRARY
Working TODAY to keep TOMORROW's future bright!

BOROUGH *of* EAST BERLIN

Historic Town Hall, Circa 1892

2014 COUNCIL MEMBERS

Charles Krall, President
James LeVan, Vice President
Andrew Raymond
Roberta Teal
Donald Dixon
Catherine Lockey
Jason Wood

Mayor Keith Hoffman

Borough Hall, Built 1975

Your East Berlin Borough Council Celebrates Our Rich History and Bright Future with You!

Civil War Reenactment

Carnival with Wagon Rides

Founder's Day Parade

Happy Anniversary

Street Pole Banner Project

Commemorative GIFTS Available!!!

Commemorating History
Est. May 8, 1764
CELEBRATE
250 YEARS
WITH US
East Berlin
Planning For The Future

Founders Day Committee

Celebrating 250 Years of East Berlin

Calendars } $15.00 Wines } $15.00 Glassware } $8.00

NELL'S FOOD MARKET

East Berlin
Pennsylvania

Richard J. Gross Post 8896
Veterans of Foreign Wars

Home and Club Association
of Post 8896

Ladies' Auxiliary
Richard J. Gross Post 8896
Veterans of Foreign Wars

WE HONOR THE DEAD
BY HELPING THE LIVING

East Berlin Beverage Dist.

(717) 259-0513 | 219 West King Street East Berlin

This Studio at Brown's Dam along the Conewago Creek was formerly operated by Osma and Milo Gallinger. It is now owned and operated by Katharine S. and Harry E. Manning. The Mannings teach Beginners, Intermediate, Advanced, and Special Techniques in Handweaving. A Beginner may come for a week or two and live right at the studio. Day students come and have access to more than twenty floor looms. They may come for instructions or to weave on any of the special warps set up at all times.

Vacation guests find this a very restful place.

Custom made linens and other handcrafted gifts and antiques for sale.

Write or call THE MANNINGS for further information.

East Berlin Area Joint Authority

Servicing East Berlin Area for Clean Water & Sewer

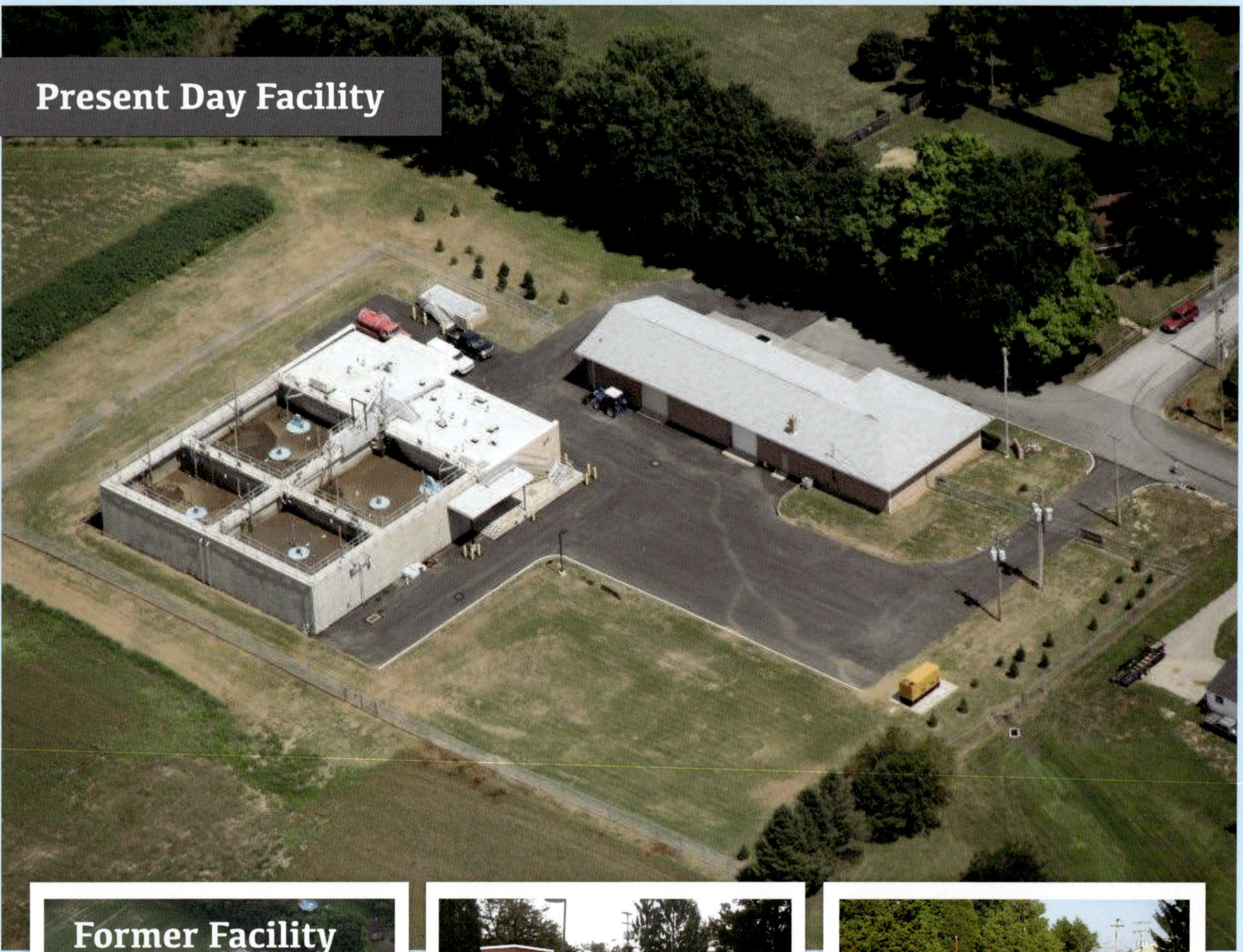

Present Day Facility

Former Facility

2009/08/26

OFFICE HOURS:
Monday-Friday
8:00 AM – 3:30 PM

CONTACT US:
717-259-8370 Phone
717-259-8372 Fax
www.ebaja12.com

BUCHART
HORN, INC.
Strengthening Communities®

Pennwood Products is situated on 16 acres in East Berlin, PA. It was founded in 1942 by Newell E. Coxon Sr. It began as a saw mill with two (2) drying kilns and woodworking equipment. During the 40's and 50's Pennwood manufactured wooden heels for ladies shoes and picture frame moldings.

Pennwood Products 1948

As the 1960s began, Newell E. "Skip" Coxon, Jr. became president and expanded the business further into products such as kitchen cabinet moldings and cabinet parts.

During the 1970's Pennwood introduced another new product line to its manufacturing facility, parquet flooring. Pennwood started its production of manufacturing parquet flooring systems under contract with Arco Chemical Corporation. This product gradually evolved into Pennwood's twelve-inch, full-perimeter tongue and groove parquet flooring. The Parquet Flooring Division was sold in 1985 to Perma Grain.

By 1980 Pennwood added another plant location and supplemented its product line with grandfather clock cases and miscellaneous furniture items. This plant was sold in 1990 to a Washington, D.C. furniture retail chain.

Today, Pennwood Products manufactures high quality, pre-finished and un-finished hardwood moldings, thin strip flooring, and premium wood fuel pellets. Our pellets are a true "green" heat source recycled from wood fibers accumulated from our sawing, machining and sanding processes.

Pennwood Products 2013

Pennwood Products remains competitive by consistently investing in our staff, equipment and technology while continuing to provide the traditional warmth and beauty of quality wood products.

We have a highly skilled and loyal workforce; some of our employees are second generation Pennwood family who are continuing the tradition of Pennwood excellence. In April of 2002, third generation, Kraig N. Coxon, joined Pennwood and serves as Executive Vice- President.

P.O. Box 766
102 Locust Street
East Berlin, PA 17316
Phone: (717) 2599551 Fax: (717) 259-7560
www.pennwoodproducts.com

Environmental Statement Pennwood Products Inc. strongly believes that proper and ethical worldwide forestry practices are important to the world's populations, to our customers, and to us. We are committed to the legal trade of timber and do not condone any illegal or unethical acquisition, transport, or documentation of wood products international or domestic. Many of Pennwood's raw materials come from Pennsylvania and surrounding states in the Appalachian mountain chain. These materials have been certified as both legal and sustainable by the USDA Forest Service.

Hanover Rental Cars | Hanover Collision and Repair

Hanover Auto Team Hanover, PA treats the needs of each individual customer with paramount concern. We know that you have high expectations, and as a car dealer we enjoy the challenge of meeting and exceeding those standards each and every time. Allow us to demonstrate our commitment to excellence!

www.hanoverautoteam.com

Congratulations

EAST BERLIN BOROUGH

ON CELEBRATING 250 YEARS!

Adams County Winery is proud to have Tears of Gettysburg and Rebel Red voted as the official wines of the East Berlin Borough's 250th Celebration.

Established in 1975, Adams County Winery was Gettysburg's first winery. Since then, our business has grown into a nationally recognized producer of award-winning wines. Our Farm Winery is located in a Civil War era Pennsylvania bank barn that is nestled against the South Mountains. We have an ideal climate for growing grapes that, in turn, make our quality wines.

Whether you're a wine connoisseur or a complete newcomer, we offer a fun, inviting, and casual atmosphere where anyone can relax, taste wine, and feel at home. We invite you to visit one of our three locations: the Farm Winery in Orrtanna, the Wine Shop at 25C in Downtown Gettysburg, or the Wine Shop at Hanover located in the Amish Markets.

717.334.4631 adamscountywinery.com

The Farm Winery
251 Peach Tree Road
Orrtanna, PA 17353

Wine Shop at 25C
25 Chambersburg Street
Gettysburg, PA 17325

Wine Shop at Hanover
located in the Amish Markets
1649 Broadway
Hanover, PA 17331

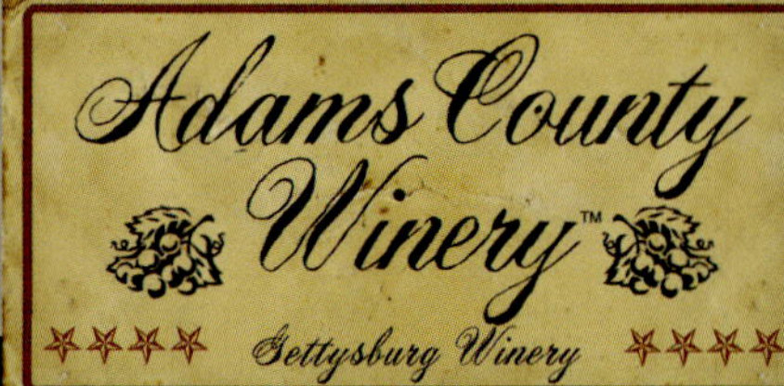

EAST BERLIN CAR WASH

406 Abbottstown St.
East Berlin, PA

EAST BERLIN LIONS CLUB

WE SERVE

Liberty

Intelligence

Our

Nation's

Safety

East Berlin Lions Club

We Serve...

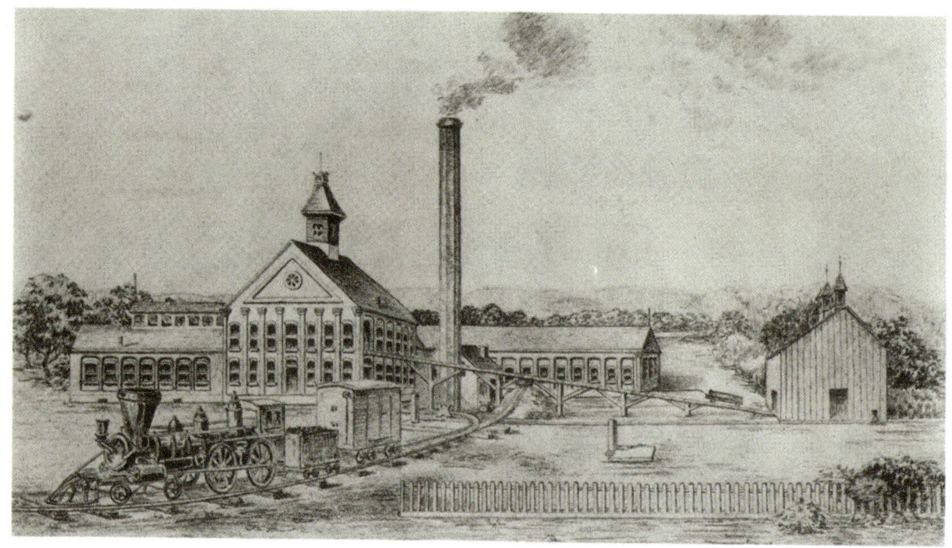

P. H. GLATFELTER CO.
IS PROUD TO SHARE
THE LAST CENTURY
WITH YOU

The P. H. Glatfelter Company in Spring Grove, Pennsylvania

Hannelore and Kenneth Furst

Mike and Shirl Thoman

Mike and Holly Cookerly

Greg and Linda Green

Jim and Noelle Kline

Gerald and Theresa Shank

Charles and Dottie Mae Eisenhart

Charles (Butch) and Venice Krall

Dave and Karen Frey

Gerald L. and Alliene K. Mummert

Brandt Ensor

Wayne and Yvonne Lau

Robbie Teal

Christopher, Andrea and TJ Teal

Mayo W. & Carol B. Bechtel

Ralph and Susie Myers

Ron and Deb Myers

Wayne and Shirley Mummert

Phil and Deb Keener and family

Donald B. Dixon

Terry and Helen Henning

Max and Emily Emig

Gerald M. and Becky Mummert

Craig, Alison and Jacob Schriver

Leslie and Annie Deardorff

Mary Beth and Jim LeVan

Bill and Carole Mayer